UnFair Lending

Why discrimination in banking still exists and how to prevent it.

Tory Haggerty

Edited by Kelli Kissack and Erica Haggerty

Cover, graphics, and book design by Jen Pfeiffer

This book is dedicated to everyone who has faced discrimination in the lending industry.

It's our constitutional right to prosper as individuals, and I'm doing my part to make that a reality.

You might be surprised to see me writing an endorsement for this book because Tory Haggerty and Tuscan Club Consulting is technically a competitor to my business. However, I consider Tory a friend and honestly, I'm proud of him for devoting the time, energy, and resources to writing this book.

Tory admits he has a "BHAG" – a Big Hairy Audacious Goal – to end discrimination in the banking industry. While that may seem like an impossible goal, I love Tory's passion and it's contagious! Why would you not want to see his BHAG accomplished too? Therefore, I hope all who pick up this book will take the time to glean from his wisdom and apply the principles he discusses within these pages. Join the "fight" to eliminate illegal discrimination. If you do, this world will be a better place. And that's a goal we should all want to achieve!

David Dickinson
Banker's Compliance Consulting

UnFair Lending is a book aimed at bringing discrimination to light in the banking and financial industry. The goal of this book is to educate and enlighten the general public on why discrimination exists, but it's also to educate those in the industry on what they can do to help solve this problem.

All of the stories in this book are first-hand accounts of examinations and audits our team has encountered throughout our careers. While Tory is the principle author of this book, he had assistance from other experts in the banking industry to bring all of these ideas together. All identities of people or organizations represented in this book are deliberately hidden.

Table of Contents

Don't Skip This Part

I want to start by telling you why I wrote this book. Discrimination in banking is as old as the industry itself. For too long, families have been denied homeownership simply because of the color of their skin. People can't get funding to start a business or go to college because of their race. Buying a home is one of the best wealth building tools available, and it can lift people and families out of generational poverty – if they are given the chance to get a loan. Unfortunately, banking products are not marketed to them, they are discouraged from applying, denied when they are otherwise creditworthy, or bank locations are not placed anywhere near where they live. Some banks are set up to avoid making loans to people of color and are unknowingly or unintentionally keeping people of color from being banked.

For too long, the industry has done too little to address this problem. Too many experts want to start a fair lending review or build a fair lending program using tools such as regression analysis, matched pairs, or a comparative file analyses. They want to use mathematical models, studies, and examples of other banks screwing up to piece together what a fair lending program should look like. These terms I've mentioned are tools that help identify discrimination, but the problem is those tools do nothing in the way of prevention. They are all reactive measures. Imagine using some mathematical tool to solely tell bank leadership that they have wide-spread discrimination. How about we instead give banks the tools to prevent it in the first place?

I'm not trying to discredit current methods of identifying discrimination in banking. What I'm saying is that rather than focusing on identification of existing problems, let's focus on prevention of future ones. I almost feel that banking discrimination is similar to working with diseases. Are healthcare providers only treating symptoms or actually going out and trying to find a cure for diseases? I feel that just treating symptoms is like identifying discrimination that has already happened. It gives us something to do, but it doesn't make progress in curing the problem. Why don't we turn our focus to prevention instead of continually identifying problems that we know are already there? In banking, few people talk about prevention as a potential cure to ending discrimination. It's time to change the way we think of our banking system. It's time to focus on prevention.

Rather than use terminology people don't understand and identification methods that make no sense to the average person, why can't we simply focus on the process of making a loan? From the moment you fill out a loan application to the final decision, there are a lot of fair lending risks along the way. What if we were to write basic procedures, train lenders on how to follow them, and then check up and make sure they are doing their jobs? Why have we made this so complicated when it can be rather simple?

I hope to answer those questions and more throughout this book, and I hope to accomplish that goal through storytelling. I've been in the banking industry for over 13 years. I started my career as a federal bank examiner and received my commission as a compliance examiner. After six years of working on nearly 100 different bank examinations, I left the federal government and went to work for a few different banks.

The problem with me working for a bank is I sucked as a banker. I didn't like the fact that I could not affect any change, and to be honest, suits are uncomfortable. That's when I decided to start my own consulting company to focus on helping banks make sense of the laws and regulations. Through the journey of building up my business of nearly 50 clients across the country, I had the chance to work on another 150 audit projects. I've seen some great examples of doing things the right way, but I've also seen a lot of great examples of doing things the wrong way. I want to share those examples with you in this book through storytelling. Some of my stories are from my days as an examiner, and some are from my days as an auditor and consultant. All of them are real-world examples, but don't worry; I have shielded the identities of the guilty parties. Well, most of them anyway.

Since I started my own business in 2017, I've also developed the nation's first commercially available fair lending school. Our school is designed to teach banking compliance and audit professionals how to conduct their own fair lending reviews. We took the best stories and materials out of that course and put them into this book. If you're interested in learning more about our fair lending school, you can find it at www.tcuniversity.us.

What if I were to tell you that most banks have never had a good quality fair lending audit? What if I were to tell you hardly anybody is talking about prevention in fair lending? I hope to change that with this book.

One of my favorite authors Jim Collins talks about his concept of BHAGs. A BHAG is a Big Hairy Audacious Goal. It's something that gets you out of bed in the morning and drives your organization forward. It's your purpose. I have a BHAG. I want to end discrimination in the banking industry. I know that sounds a bit out-of-reach. I mean seriously, what chance does a middle-aged white guy living in the Midwest have to end centuries old discrimination in a multi-trillion-dollar industry? I guess when you put it that way, it sounds hard. Yes, the odds are stacked against me, and I don't know how far I will get, but I'm going to try. I'm going to do my part, and this book is a continuation of that journey.

Our mission is to end discrimination in the banking industry.

If you want to learn about why discrimination in the banking industry still exists and what we can do to prevent it, you have come to the right place. I want to empower you with more knowledge and some hope. If you're a banker, I want to share some specific insights on changes you can consider right away at your bank. If you're a person who knows little on this topic, I want you to walk away armed with tools to help identify discrimination you otherwise would not have seen.

Many of the ideas in this book are quite simple, but actually putting these ideas into motion can be challenging. Think about it in the same way as wanting to lose weight. You know that eating healthier and exercising can easily help you to lose weight. Those are simple solutions, but actually following through with it is the hard part. It's difficult to lose weight when sodas, pizza, and cake are so delicious. It's also hard to build a lending program free of discrimination when you're just out to make money. Our battle after reading this book is the follow through.

I also want to make sure you have an open mind when you read this book. If you are a banker, I don't care if you have been in banking for 30 years or 30 minutes. There likely will be concepts that are new to you or you will find new ways to look at old concepts. I don't pretend to have all of the answers, but many of the ideas we will talk about are new, and it's important to be open to new ways of looking at a very old problem.

I want you to walk away from this book inspired, better educated, and have some relief that there are simple steps you can take that will make an impact. This is a major problem, and it's going to take a lot of inspired people to make real change happen. Let's go!

Part 1

FAIR LENDING OVERVIEW

CHAPTER ONE

What is Fair Lending and Why Does it Matter?

The million-dollar question; what exactly is fair lending? The U.S. Department of Housing and Urban Development (HUD) says that "fair lending prohibits lenders from considering your race, color, national origin, religion, sex, familial status, or disability when applying for residential mortgage loans. Fair lending guarantees the same lending opportunities to everyone." I have different definition.

Fair lending is the process of making consistent loan decisions based on someone's creditworthiness and not their personal characteristics.

Fair lending is so much more than a list of personal characteristics you can't use in loan decisions. Unfortunately, fair lending has a bad stigma in our country, and people get so scared of the consequences for not treating people fairly. What if I was to tell you that there is a simple method of treating people fairly that every bank can implement? It's not rocket science. Most banks have already implemented many of the ideas that I will talk about in this book. However, a weak lending program and poor training is usually what gets banks into trouble.

I want to go through a couple quick stories and talk about a few myths. People outside of the industry (and many bankers themselves) have these ideas about what fair lending really means. Let me share three brief stories with you to get started on explaining what fair lending is and what it is not.

Fair Lending Myths

I once did a review of a bank where we tested how they were pricing car loans to male and female applicants. This bank had about 10 different markets where their branches were located. Each of the market presidents had the authority to reduce the interest rate on the loan as they saw fit. People ask all of the time if their bank can match the interest rate of the bank down the street, and these individuals have the power to do that.

In a nutshell, they were supposed to price loans based on an approved interest rate sheet, but the market presidents were allowed to make their own adjustments. This itself increases risk of lending fairly, but the bigger issue was that there was no real guidance on how much or how often they should adjust the interest rate. Every market president was just left to do their own thing, and management just hoped for the best, I guess.

We did some testing and found out that one branch in particular was charging more than a 2% higher interest rate for car loans to women than to men. This was a big red flag, so we investigated even further into the data. What we found was that it was two specific female lenders that were causing problems. Women lenders were discriminating against other women by charging them much higher interest rates to buy a car than men with the same creditworthiness.

Lending Myth #1:
People don't discriminate against those with whom they share common characteristics. They do – and often.

I once came across a bank that had made significantly less home loans to minority applicants than to white applicants. Based on the percentage of minority people that lived in their market area, those minority applicants should have had significantly more loans. The bank had never reviewed any of the data, so they had no idea that not only were they not making loans to minority applicants, they were also not receiving any applications from them.

It's hard to make loans to a group of people that never apply for them. How can a bank not know this information? Strange, right? It happens all of the time.

Lending Myth #2:
If data is available, people will look at it.
Wrong again. Many banks have never done
a quality internal fair lending audit.

I once partnered with a client in a rural part of the Midwest. If you know anything about this part of the country, the minority population is low and even more so in rural areas. There were very few people of color in the community where this bank was located.

This bank had an African-American gentleman come in and apply for an unsecured consumer loan. He wanted to borrow $1,000, but he didn't have anything to offer as collateral if he didn't pay back the loan. These are very high-risk loans for a bank to make. This man didn't even have a checking account, and there was no car or home to repossess if he didn't pay back the loan. When they pulled his credit score, it was barely 500. If you don't know anything about credit scores, that number is bad and well below the score a normal lender would accept when lending money without any collateral.

I know what some of you may be thinking. I would not give somebody with a documented history of not paying his bills $1,000 with no collateral, and you would be right to make that decision. Unfortunately, that is not what happened. This was a small town, and he was one of the only persons of color who lived there. The bank president was so worried about fair lending and discrimination that against his better judgment, he made this gentleman the loan. Not surprisingly, the applicant with a 500-credit score and a long history of poorly handling credit did not repay his loan. That $1,000 walked out the door and was never seen again.

Lending Myth #3:
There are laws that say when banks must make loans.
You guessed it – wrong again. There are laws that prevent discrimination, but they don't force you to make bad loans.

The Root Cause

What is common among these three stories? There may be several things that you can tie together, but the thing I see is a lack of education and training. It's bank managers who don't understand how to build a simple fair lending program. It's compliance teams not knowing how to test their lender's performance. So many banks have poor policies and procedures and lack simple guidelines on how to make safe but fair loans.

I have traveled all over the upper Midwest and trained thousands of lenders, compliance and audit professionals, and bank executives on these basic fair lending principles. One of my favorite things to do is to start each of my training sessions with a quiz question.

True or false: A bank can legally discriminate against a loan applicant.

I know that may sound a bit ridiculous at the moment. You may be shouting out the answer right now or wondering why I would ask such a dumb question. I really love asking this question in live training sessions to see how people react and see how many brave souls dare to raise their hands. Keep that question in the back of your mind as we will revisit that in a later chapter.

Throughout this book, I will introduce you to what I call the loan life cycle of risks. There are several processes that lenders complete when making a loan to an applicant. Each one of those processes have different fair lending risks associated with them. As a whole, banks need to put a program in place to ensure that they are treating all applicants fairly and consistently according to the law. It may seem complicated and a difficult task, but it's not as difficult as you might think.

Chapter Takeaways

- Fair lending is building a program to treat everyone consistently.
- People discriminate against others who share common characteristics.
- Many banks have never completed a good quality fair lending audit.

The Details

For those of you in the banking industry looking for more meat behind these concepts, I'm going to have a details section at the end of each chapter. I want to dive a bit deeper and give you more to think about. Let's get into the details.

I've heard a thousand times from a thousand bankers that since compliance handles fair lending that it's a compliance problem. Commercial lenders are the worst at thinking that compliance issues don't apply to them. If that's really true, then riddle me this: Compliance Officers don't make loans! Fair lending is not a compliance problem – it's a lender problem. Because of this, you will need the lender's help to solve it.

When you do your reviews, don't play favorites with lenders or make snap judgments. One of the takeaways of this chapter is thinking that just because someone shares common characteristics means they won't discriminate. I've seen firsthand, more than once, loan officers of color discriminate against applicants of color. We already talked about women discriminating against other women. Do not assume that just because your lender is a certain race, ethnicity, or sex that you "don't need to worry about them." Make sure you remain objective throughout your entire review. You just never know where you will find discrimination.

CHAPTER TWO

Laws and Regulations

Do not let the chapter title intimidate you. We are going to talk about laws and regulations, and I will admit that can be boring. But, it's important. This sets the table for what banks can and cannot do. You may be surprised to learn that there are not that many laws, and there's not much to them. You may be even more surprised to hear that there is no "fair lending" law or regulation. That's right. One of the biggest risk areas that scares most bank executives has little formal guidance. How can we possibly build a fair lending program around a regulation that does not exist? Well, that's one of the reasons we're in this mess. I want you to think of fair lending as a group of concepts and rules that banks are supposed to build their programs around.

The fact that there is no one-stop shop of what you need to do is a likely reason that so many bankers in the industry are lost on this topic. A nice little roadmap can go a long way to helping bankers out, so let's try and build one.

Equal Credit Opportunity Act

There are laws and regulations that exist that help guide us on not necessarily what to do, but what not to do. The most important of these is the Equal Credit Opportunity Act, or ECOA. While this may sound like some long and expansive law that provides thousands of pages of guidance to the banking industry, the basic concept is actually short and quite simple. The biggest takeaway is what they call the prohibited bases, some of which you have already learned.

Lenders are not allowed to use a prohibited basis characteristic when making a loan decision, but what is a "prohibited basis"? Think of it as a personal characteristic in which you often have little to no control over. The use of prohibited bases is tied to these personal characteristics.

ECOA has nine prohibited bases that every lender must follow. Lenders cannot make a loan decision on any of the following characteristics of a loan applicant:

- Race
- Color
- Religion
- Sex
- National origin
- **Age**
- **Marital status**
- **Applicant's receipt of income derived from any public assistance program**
- **Applicant's exercise, in good faith, of any right under the Consumer Credit Protection Act**

Lenders are not allowed to use a prohibited basis group characteristics in making a loan decision.

This may sound like a simple list, and generally it is, but this is our baseline for making loans fairly. A lender simply cannot consider somebody's race, sex, or age when making a loan decision. Another important factor to point out is that ECOA's prohibited bases are applicable to every type of loan, not just consumer loans. That means that a financial institution cannot use these bases in loan decisions for business loans, credit cards, home loans, car loans, farm loans, and any other loan type you can think of.

The prohibited basis characteristics have nothing to do with a customer's ability to repay a loan.

Fair Housing Act

There is one more key law that is very similar to ECOA, and it is the Fair Housing Act, or FHA. There are two main differences between the ECOA and the FHA. While the ECOA covers all loan types, the FHA, as its name implies, is strictly for home loans, although it has other applications in other industries.

The FHA also has a list of prohibited bases that are very similar to the ECOA. In fact, the first five are exactly the same:

- Race
- Color
- Religion
- Sex
- National origin
- **Familial status**
- **Handicap**

You will notice the last two are different. As you may have guessed, if you are getting a home loan, both lists of prohibited bases will apply.

Home Mortgage Disclosure Act

There are other laws that also have an impact on fair lending from which we borrow guidance. The next one I want to discuss is the Home Mortgage Disclosure Act, or HMDA (often pronounced "hum-duh"). This law requires data collection on home loans for certain lenders. This law doesn't necessarily tell you what you cannot do like ECOA and FHA, rather it requires banks to collect pieces of data on home loan applications and the people who apply. Not all lenders have to collect HMDA data. There are size requirements, loan volumes, and branch location requirements that trigger a lender to have to collect and report home loan data. Many banks are required to collect and report HMDA data but not all banks fall into that category.

HMDA requires certain banks to collect information on people who apply for a home loan.

You're probably thinking "Wait a minute" and for good reason. I just got done telling you that banks cannot use your personal characteristics (prohibited bases) when making home loans, and now I'm telling you that they are required by law to collect that data when you apply for one. So why on earth would they be collecting the information they cannot legally use?

The answer is actually for the opposite reason. It is so that bank examiners can use the information to test and verify that banks are not using that information when making home loan decisions. By knowing those prohibited basis characteristics for all home loan applicants, banking regulators can test to see if banks are treating all applicants fairly or differently on a prohibited basis. When you think about it, how can you know if a bank treats people of different races fairly if you have no idea the race of the people getting loans?

Community Reinvestment Act

Another major law that has some fair lending impact is the Community Reinvestment Act, or CRA. The CRA tests whether or not banks are reinvesting into the communities in which they operate. Some of the discussions and loan life cycle risks that we will talk about in this book are directly related to the CRA.

One of the good things about the CRA (or bad depending on who you ask) is that the findings are public information. A bank's CRA Performance Evaluation can be easily found online. That means the average person can look to see how a bank has performed and whether or not they are meeting the needs of their community.

CRA ratings are public information and can be found online for all banks in the US through their primary regulator's website.

CRA performance doesn't line up exactly with fair lending, so it's important not to confuse the two. If a bank has a bad CRA rating, that doesn't necessarily mean it is discriminating but could just mean that it is not lending enough to its own market area.

I realize that for the average person, learning about laws and regulations is not the most exciting topic. However, you will need to understand the basics of these laws so that we can apply the concepts to a fair lending program. One of the reasons why fair lending is confusing and difficult for most banks to master is because there is no overarching law or regulation. There's no easy play book to follow. We have to understand all of the laws that have fair lending impact and somehow piece them together to ensure that we treat loan applicants fairly.

Chapter Takeaways:

- The ECOA and FHA established prohibited basis groups, and banks cannot use those characteristics in making loan decisions.
- The HMDA requires certain lenders to collect data on home loan applicants to help regulators find discrimination.
- The CRA helps determine if banks are meeting the credit needs of their areas.

The Details:

ECOA and FHA and the prohibited bases are a good start, but there is much more to a fair lending program than a list of words. You will want to think about the prohibited basis groups when reviewing your entire loan program, including the loan lifecycle concepts that we will introduce in the next chapter.

If you're a HMDA reporter, it's critical that you get fair lending software to analyze your HMDA data. You already know the importance of scrubbing your data to ensure it's accurate, but you need to follow that same mentality when reviewing the data. Good fair lending software should be able to give you detailed reports on many of the loan lifecycle risks we will cover.

Make sure you actually know how to use the software! I know that sounds silly, but I've had many clients that pay thousands of dollars a year for fair lending software but have no idea how to use it. If you're not getting the customer service you need from your current vendor, it might be time to look for other options.

The CRA is a good starting point to see how you are performing, but the borrower profile and geographic distribution loan tests under the CRA only focus on lending to low- and moderate-income (LMI) people and areas. Just because you got a satisfactory or even an outstanding rating on your last CRA performance evaluation doesn't mean you're not discriminating. That just means you're lending to LMI people and areas, or you had really outstanding community development activities. Fair lending looks at LMI people and areas, but more importantly it looks at minority people and areas, something the CRA doesn't consider.

CHAPTER THREE

Loan Lifecycle of Fair Lending Risks

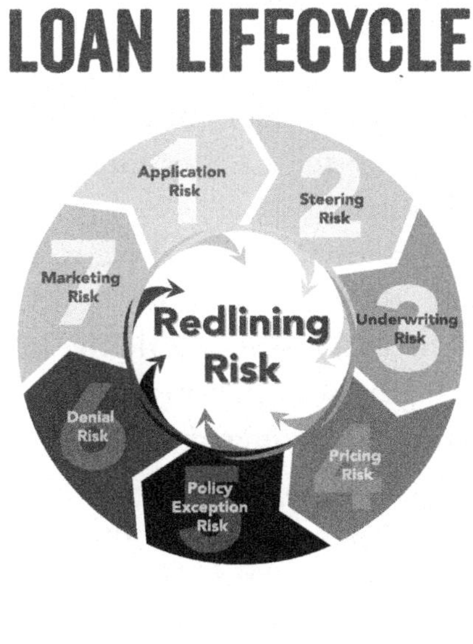

Every bank has some type of informal procedure when it comes to applying for a loan, but the basic steps are the same. Imagine walking into your local bank branch. The first thing you will do is sit down with a lender and fill out an application. They likely will ask you some questions and help you find the loan product that meets your needs. If you are applying for car loan at a dealership, you may even get the pleasure of hearing about their extended warranty program. This is called an add-on product.

Once they collect all of your data, they will have to make the loan decision or underwrite the loan. Sometimes you may not meet all of the criteria they are looking for, so they might have to get an exception to policy approved. In other instances, your application may be denied.

If you get approved, then they need to set the terms of the loan like the rate, any fees, and how long you have to repay. Even then they may look for policy exceptions if you are trying to negotiate for a better interest rate than what they are currently offering.

You may have noticed on the drive to the bank a billboard advertising their products or heard a commercial about them on the radio. Even inside the lobby or at your lender's desk, you may see other marketing materials about current specials they have going on. You also may notice that you had to travel a long way to get to a bank branch or you may notice that there are few, if any, branches in your area. These are the loan lifecycle of risks. Every step in that process has risks tied to it.

While banks have different ways of making loans, they all generally follow the loan lifecycle concept.

In this chapter, I will lay out the foundation or building blocks for the loan life cycle concept. I want you to think of all these risks separately, but as we get through each one, we will also start piecing them together. All of the risks combined make up what a fair lending program should be built around.

LOAN LIFECYCLE

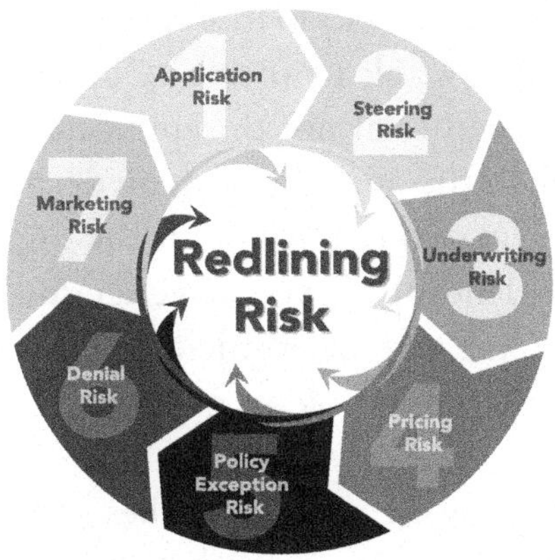

Application Risk – There are two risks to think about during the application process: the actual physical application that customers fill out and a bank's process for taking applications. You may be thinking how could something so simple like taking an application present any fair lending risk? There are a lot of ways to screw this up, and we will get into that a little later.

Steering Risk – Most banks will offer more than a single loan product. While banks don't have to offer every type of loan product ever created, it's good for customers to have options. How a customer gets into a certain loan product is steering. Lenders will help customers find the right product that fits their needs. This can be a good thing. A bank that gets a customer into the best product that meets their needs is going to be successful. When is it a bad thing? When it is done on a prohibited basis. How banks and lenders sell add-on products is another major risk that we have already mentioned.

Underwriting Risk – Underwriting is a fancy term for the process of making the loan decision. A lender or underwriter will analyze all of the facts of a loan application and determine whether or not the applicant is qualified for a loan. This is when the approve or deny decision is made. As you may have guessed, this is one of the biggest risks when it comes to fair lending. If you have lenders denying loans based on someone's race or ethnicity, that's about as simple and big as fair lending problems get.

Pricing Risk – Once a lender takes an application, gets the applicant into the best product for their needs, and makes the approval decision, they must price the loan. What is pricing? The most obvious part of the price of a loan is the interest rate. However, there is more to pricing than just the rate. The fees a customer is charged can be a significant portion of the loan cost. There are also other things to consider such as the loan term or how much time you get to repay the loan.

Policy Exception Risk – Every financial institution should have basic procedures on how to fairly and consistently make loan decisions and price loans. In other words, a lender should know what credit score you need to qualify for a loan. They shouldn't be guessing. They should also have guidance on what rate you qualify for. However, lenders will often go outside of official bank policy. That is how policy exceptions are born.

Let's say your credit score is just below the minimum required score but you get the loan anyway – a policy exception has happened. When a lender approves a loan that bank policy says should be denied, lenders are essentially writing new policy. Done rarely, this poses little risk. Done often, it creates a ton of fair lending risk.

Denial Risk – We know that not every loan application is going to be approved. If a bank approved every loan application that came through the door, they would lose a lot of money. Every person has the right to apply for a loan, but not every person will qualify. The denial process is the last lender decision step in the loan life cycle, and it is very much tied to underwriting risk. If a bank has strong underwriting guidance that is always followed, they don't have to worry about much when it comes to who they approve and who they deny for a loan. If they have poor underwriting guidance or lenders never follow it, denial risk increases dramatically.

Marketing Risk – The advertising and marketing messages that a bank puts out to customers are likely the first time the customers will hear about a bank's products and services. There are many different ways for banks to advertise their products. For larger banks, television is more common. Smaller banks and those in rural communities tend to do more print and radio advertising.

Nearly all banks use social media and paid online ads. Both can be a good thing, but they bring on a ton of new risks. Banks not only have to worry about the message itself and what they are saying but who is targeted to actually see and hear it. Marketing is really the first risk in the loan lifecycle process, but we'll look at it at the end. I want to discuss the other risks and then wrap up the life cycle with marketing.

Redlining Risk – There is one major risk that is very much part of the loan life cycle, but it is more of a larger concept in lending. The simplest way to describe redlining is when a bank does not provide equal access to loans based on geography.

Some banks have refused to make loans in certain neighborhoods, and it's not a coincidence that those neighborhoods have higher minority populations. We see this happen the most in home loan lending, but any loan product can have redlining risk. Small business lending is another great example where we can find redlining problems.

As I mentioned in the introduction, for a large majority of Americans, their home will be their single biggest purchase they will ever make. When banks intentionally or unintentionally refuse to make home loans in certain areas, those areas cannot prosper. A family owning a home is one of the simplest ways to get out of poverty. When families are restricted from home ownership, they suffer. This problem is then passed down to their children and leads to generational poverty.

There are other factors to consider when it comes to a fair lending program, but these loan life cycle risks makeup a substantial majority of a bank's fair lending troubles. Banks must not only understand these risks but put a program in place to mitigate them.

Chapter Takeaways

- The loan lifecycle is the process of a person applying for and receiving a loan from a bank.
- Each of the loan lifecycle processes has its unique fair lending risks.
- No matter the bank or their size, everyone goes through the loan lifecycle process.

The Details

You should be building your compliance and fair lending programs around each of the loan lifecycle risks. You should have policies and procedures to guide your employees for all of these risks. Make sure you train your loan staff about how to make a fair loan decision at your bank. Don't worry if you don't know what to do just yet. We will get more in-depth as we examine each of the loan lifecycle risks.

Part 2

LOAN LIFECYCLE

CHAPTER FOUR

Application Risk

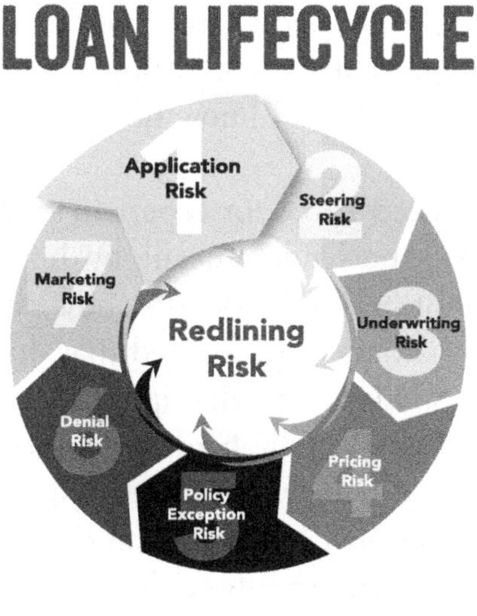

The Complaint

During my days as an FDIC bank examiner, we had a complaint come through our office. The complaint was from a customer of a bank that we supervised. It just so happened that we were getting ready to do a routine examination of the bank, and that included a fair lending review.

The complaint went something like this. A female minority applicant went into this bank to apply for a car loan. This was a pretty small bank. They only had one location in a small town and just two loan officers. The loan officer that the complaint was against was a white male lender. During the conversation, the applicant indicated that she wanted to apply for a loan so that she could buy a car for her family. The lender's response was "I know how you people are with car loans."

You do not need to be an expert in discrimination to understand what the lender meant by his comment. He felt that people of her race shouldn't buy cars because of a predetermined bias, and he vocalized that during the application process. Spoiler alert: the applicant was not happy. Not surprisingly, she left the bank without completing the application process. Shortly after, she filed a discrimination complaint that eventually ended up on our desk.

Since we were getting ready to do the fair lending exam, that complaint played a big part in what we were going to review. We decided not to look at their loan decision process (underwriting), or how they set interest rates (pricing), or if they were lending to all parts of the community (redlining). We focused on that complaint, that lender, and that prohibited basis characteristic.

One complaint can be the focus of an entire fair lending examination.

The point of this story is that complaints matter, and fair lending complaints matter even more. Regulators take them very seriously, and we dug deep to find out just how widespread the problem was. Filing a complaint directly to the bank may or may not result in action. Filing a complaint directly to the bank's regulator is a much different story.

Through many interviews, reviews of other applications and loans that lender made, and follow-up letters to and from the applicant, we were able to determine that there wasn't more widespread discrimination. The lender made many loans to that prohibited basis group and at the same terms and rates as white applicants.

Writing Basic Procedures

There are still a lot of problems with this situation. This particular lender had predetermined biases. In addition, the bank lacked basic application procedures. That brings us to our first risk in the loan life cycle: application risk.

Every bank should consider some basic procedures on how to take a loan application.

If we are talking about a small bank with only a few branches and lenders, these procedures can be informal. As the size of a bank grows, formal controls and procedures become more critical.

Let's move away from focusing on just lenders for a moment. What I want you to understand is that the application process extends beyond just the loan officer. Banks need to train lenders on fair lending, but lenders are not the only bank employees who create application risk.

Let's discuss a different but similar scenario. Let's imagine a white male applicant walks into any random bank in the United States. He strolls up to the teller line and says "I want to apply for a car loan." The teller greets him with a smile and says "Certainly. Here's an application. Please take a seat, fill it out, and I will get a lender to assist you." There's nothing wrong with that procedure. It sounds fairly standard and harmless and probably happens every day in this country.

Now let's imagine that later in the same day a minority applicant walks up to that same teller and says "I want to apply for a car loan." The same teller hands the minority applicant the same paper application but this time says "Please fill out this application and mail it in." Did that teller just treat two applicants differently? The more important question is, did they just treat them differently because of a prohibited basis (race)? Banks need to train all customer-facing personnel on the basics of the loan application process.

Any person in a bank that interacts directly with customers (even on the phone) has the opportunity to discriminate, whether intentional or not.

Screening Applicants

The second application risk is when loan officers screen people and discourage them from ever applying in the first place. It's a common practice for a loan officer to ask basic questions while taking a loan application. There is nothing wrong with this. The process helps the lender determine what product is a best fit, if the applicant has collateral, or what they would likely qualify for. The problem lies when a lender then starts making informal credit decisions and when they think someone doesn't qualify, convinces the applicant to withdraw the application.

Imagine having a conversation with a lender who asks you an estimate of your credit score. If you know your credit score is very low, the lender may tell you that you are likely not going to qualify, so you decide not to apply. This is an everyday example of discouraging applications. Based on the size of a bank, it's not hard to see how many applications they took in a year and how many denials they had. When the number of denials is unusually low, it raises red flags that this can be occurring.

Very low denial rates can be an indicator that lenders are screening people and discouraging them from applying.

I also want to point out though that it's entirely possible that lenders are just not doing their jobs of going through the denial process. That process does require more work. Or, lenders can just shred an application and pretend it doesn't exist. Either way, not keeping an accurate record of denials causes more harm than good because it's a major red flag for potential fair lending issues.

Consistent Treatment

The final piece of the application process I want to discuss is going the extra mile for one applicant but not another. Let's imagine a young man applying for a credit card. This young man has a judgment on his credit bureau report that is causing him to get denied for the credit card. The lender tells the young man that if he can pay off that judgment and come back in a month, they will rerun his credit and possibly get him approved.

Around the same time, a young lady applies for the same credit card with a similar judgment preventing her approval. The same lender simply denies her application without giving her the same chance they gave the male applicant to pay it off and reapply. Did that lender just treat people differently on a prohibited basis? The final point of the application process is that banks should treat everyone the same way every time.

Lenders should not go the extra mile for one applicant if they are not willing to do it for all applicants.

There is nothing wrong with going above and beyond to serve customers and get people loans, but it must be done fairly and consistently.

Building Prevention Into the Application Process

Banks need to establish a combination of having good procedures and training employees. All banks should have some basic application procedures. The larger the bank, the more formal they should be.

In addition, lenders need to actually be trained on the procedures. I know this sounds a bit silly, but I can't tell you how many times I've read through a wonderful procedural document. You likely have them where you work, no matter what line of business you're in. It's a nice little checklist or steps on how to do your job. The problem? Either nobody knows it exists or they just don't follow it! You will hear that theme a lot during the loan life cycle. Having good procedures is great, but they are useless if nobody knows about them or follows them.

The next step a bank needs to take is train – not only on the application procedures but on the risks we discussed. It's okay for a lender to have an informal interview with a potential loan applicant. It is not okay for them to convince someone to not apply if they think they would be denied. All applicants should be encouraged to apply for a loan and let the underwriting process (which we will talk about soon) take place.

Lastly, banks need to review their data. If banks have hardly any denials, there's likely an issue. The average consumer may look at a bank rarely denying a loan as a good thing. You may think "That is a great bank because they are giving everyone a loan and rarely denying anyone." However, it's actually a big red flag that something else is going on. If a bank makes thousands of loans a year and rarely ever denies an application, they are either not reporting their denials or screening applicants and convincing them to withdraw their application. There's no fancy conspiracy theory behind that – it's the simple law of probability.

Chapter Takeaways

- Set up basic procedures for all employees to follow when taking an application.
- Train all customer-facing employees on how to treat loan applicants fairly and consistently.
- Make sure lenders are not screening applicants and encouraging them to withdraw their applications.
- Monitor denial rates: if your denial rates are very low compared to application rates, that's a potential red flag.

The Details

There are a couple ways to dig deeper into the application process. My favorite is through lender interviews. You may have seen them as part of regulatory exams. Bank examiners often do fair lending interviews with members of the lending team to understand how they take applications.

Conducting a fair lending interview is not difficult. You do your research and read through policies and procedures. You first need to understand how lenders are supposed to make loans at your bank. Then, you just sit back, play dumb, and ask simple questions. "Tell me how you take an application," and just let the lender talk. What they tell you should match what's in your procedures. If it doesn't, you have training issues.

The other critical area you will want to monitor is denial rates. You should monitor your adverse action notices to see if your denial rates make sense. You also can monitor rates by branch, but more importantly you can track by lender. Whenever the issue arises of low denial rates, it's typically not every lender. It's usually just a few or even one. If you have lenders who take hundreds of applications a year, and most of them typically have 30 or 40 denials in that same timeframe, one lender with two denials should stand out as a red flag.

Finally, if you really suspect a problem, you can set up a secret shopper. Have people apply with that lender that likely wouldn't get approved to see if your lenders are discouraging applications. I realize this sounds like a bit of a drastic measure, but if you suspect you have this issue, it's a good way to verify.

As always, anytime you find issues, you need to go back and address the root cause. If it's bad procedures, make them better. If you have great procedures but they are not being followed, do more training. Any major weaknesses should be traced back to a root cause, and that's likely a weak element in your compliance management system. Address the root cause and monitor going forward to make sure the issue has been fixed.

CHAPTER FIVE

Steering Risk

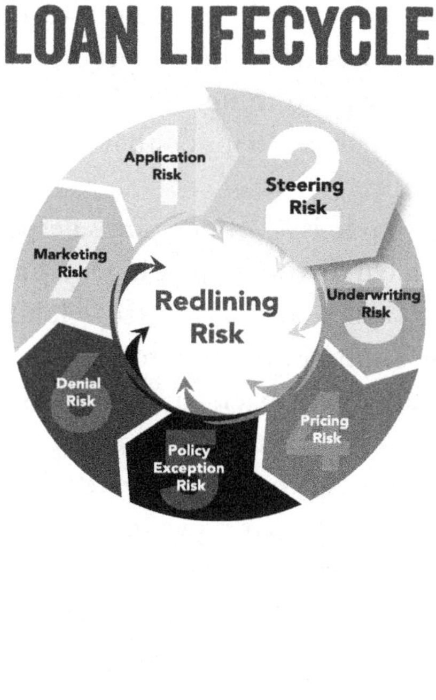

I bet you like options. Maybe you're a Double Stuf Oreo person? Or, maybe you are like me and like just a reasonable amount of "stuf"? Maybe you don't like "stuf" at all and would prefer vegetables? These are all options of things you can eat. Options are good.

Banks give you options, too, and that's also good. If you're going to buy a home, you need to decide how long you want to pay back the loan. Maybe you don't have much money down, so you get a government guaranteed loan. How about credit cards. You may have options on cash back or rewards points. You may have options about what loan product to get when buying a car. Deciding what product to get a customer into is where steering comes in. It's when a lender "steers" a customer into a product that best meets their needs. That's a good thing. We all want the best option. However, it doesn't always happen that way. We will get back to that in a minute.

Let's call it like it is – lenders are salespeople. Yes, they are the ones at a bank who help you get a loan, but they are also selling the bank's main product – loans. Banks make their money by taking in money from those who have extra (deposits) and lending it back to those who need it (loans). They charge more interest on loans than they pay out in deposits, and that margin is their profit. If you want to get more technical, we call that a net interest margin. Take the average rate they charge for money (loans) and subtract the average rate they pay for money (deposits), and you find that margin. There are other ways they also make profits, but lending is the main way for nearly all institutions.

Loan officers are also part of a bank's frontline personnel that help bring customers in. This book is definitely not an attack on loan officers. Without them, banks would not survive. When the loan officer understands their customers and gets the customer into the best loan product that meets their needs, a successful transaction has happened.

That's what steering is all about. A loan officer needs to get their customers into the right product. When a loan officer gets a customer into a product for the wrong reasons, it could potentially be a fair lending issue.

Illegal steering happens when a loan officer gets a customer into a product based on a prohibited basis.

This usually happens because of several reasons that we will cover in this chapter.

Product Options

The actual loan products that a bank offers present steering risk. I like to use an example that has three different loan products when I talk about steering risk.

Let's first imagine Loan Product A. Loan Product A has the lowest fees, the lowest interest rates, and is designed for the highest creditworthy individuals. These are customers with the highest credit scores and strongest repayment ability. They put money down on purchases, have plenty of income to pay their debts, and always pay on time. Banks love these customers for obvious reasons. Lenders find it is easy to lend high creditworthy people money because they have an established history of paying it back. They present the lowest risk to losing money, so they pay less in interest and fees.

Loan Product B is the middle-of-the-road product. The interest rates and fees are a bit higher on this loan product than Loan Product A. The loan terms are not quite as long, so payments are going to be higher. Customers who qualify for Loan Product B are not the best rated customers, but they do qualify for a decent product. Loan Product B is a good product, but it's not the best product.

Loan Product C is designed for your least creditworthy customers. In years past, the industry used to call these subprime borrowers, but that terminology is not used as commonly anymore. Loan Product C has by far the highest interest rates and highest fees. It also usually has the shortest terms to pay back the loan.

The longer you give someone to pay back a loan, the more risk you take because bad things can and do happen.

Customers that only qualify for Loan Product C are often lucky to even get a loan. They represent the highest risk. Their credit scores are the lowest that a bank is willing to accept. They often carry more debt, which means they have less income to pay back the loan, and they likely don't put any money down when they purchase an item. They are still creditworthy, but they carry the most risk.

There is nothing wrong with having three different types of loan products. If you think about how we describe them, people will fit into one of the three buckets. If they don't, they will likely get denied. So where does the fair lending risk for steering come from?

Wrong Product for the Wrong Reasons

The problem is that customers don't always get offered the best quality loan product that they qualify for. What often happens is certain borrowers, usually minority and women borrowers, get placed into Loan Products B or C when they actually qualify for something better. This is where the prohibited bases come into play and the fair lending risk grows.

A bank's compliance and audit personnel should be testing to see if applicants are being put into the loan product based on their creditworthiness. Sometimes this is very easy to do. Here's an example. Let's say you need a 720-credit score to qualify for Loan Product A. Using this criterion, you can easily see if somebody who got a loan product should or should not have received it. I can look through a list of approved loans and simply cross reference the borrower's credit score with the loan product they received.

What we often find happening is minority and female applicants are disproportionately being sold Loan Product C while non-Hispanic, white, and male applicants are being sold Loan Product A.

Loan Referral Programs

The same concept applies to loan referral programs. Banks will often work with another company (usually called a third party) to provide loan products to their customers. If a bank has a referral channel, they will need to understand the credit products that the third party offers.

For example, if a lender is always referring minority applicants to one lending channel that has much higher interest rates and fees and refers white applicants to a different lending channel that has lower rates and fees, the same steering risk is still present even though it's not the bank's own product. The actual loan product you get is only one part of steering risk. Other products a bank tries to sell you can also carry this risk. Let's change it up a bit and offer an example that you have likely experienced yourself.

Add-On Products

If you have ever bought a car and financed it through a dealership, you have likely experienced someone selling you an add-on product.

Add-on products are those extra items that come with a loan that have potential benefits.

I use the term benefits lightly because of my own personal biases on how much of a benefit they are, but that's beside the point.

A very common add-on product in a car loan transaction would be a vehicle warranty. I would like to tell you that if you turn down that vehicle warranty, those weekly calls to your phone that your vehicle warranty is expired will stop. Unfortunately, that is not likely. But on a serious note, if people are targeted for add-on products on a prohibited basis, you may have increased steering risk. Car dealerships and banks can target minority individuals with these costly add-on products and may cross a prohibited basis line.

Other examples of add-on products are credit life and

credit disability insurance. For an additional fee, sometimes quite a large fee, you can have these products "added" onto your loan. What are credit life and disability insurance?

The idea behind these products is that if you were to die (credit life insurance) or become disabled (credit disability insurance) during the loan term, the insurance will kick in and pay off your loan balance. Personally, I am not a big fan of these products. They are very expensive and rarely ever provide actual value. In all the years I have been in banking, I've heard only a select few stories of somebody having actually benefited from these products.

What increases the steering risk on these products is that the lender often receives a commission for selling this insurance. Usually, the commission for each loan may not be that high, but if you sell a lot of insurance, it can add up. Because of the risk, many institutions do not even offer this product.

Minorities applicants are frequent targets of add-on products.

Real-World Example

During a routine FDIC bank examination, our team discovered an extremely high rate of credit life insurance sales to a group of Native American borrowers. This bank was near a reservation, so it's not out of the ordinary that they had many Native American customers. What was out of the ordinary is that Native American customers made up nearly all of credit life policies sold. They were only a small percentage of total population, but they had purchased nearly every credit life policy the bank sold that year. Because of this red flag, credit life insurance sales were the focus of that fair lending examination.

I know what you might be thinking – this bank is targeting people on a prohibited basis (race) to sell them this product. At first, that's how it appeared. But there is a reason why we do the actual reviews. Just because a particular prohibited basis group appears to be experiencing discrimination doesn't mean it's true. Let's look at what we found.

During the review, we discovered that nearly every single Native American loan customer purchased credit life insurance from this bank. In fact, only one Native American customer did not purchase the insurance during the review period. That person was above the age limit to sell the product to. At first glance, it appeared that lenders were targeting Native American customers for this add-on product.

Fortunately, just because something looks bad does not mean that it is.

If you are a banker reading this book, you may feel that the examiners are always out to get you. I can promise you, they are not (Well, I guess I can only say I was not). Federal bank examiners are there to identify risk of harm to consumers. When heightened risk is found, they search for a reasonable explanation. That's exactly what our team did.

Through further research and discussions, we learned that there was a cultural impact on the high rate of credit life sales to the tribal population. The tribe's culture and teachings were to not leave debt behind to your family members when you die. Therefore, they always asked for the credit life insurance to ensure that their family members did not have to worry about debt upon their death. This situation is a perfect example of how something can appear to be an issue, yet there is a plausible and legal explanation.

How to Find Steering Risk

How does a bank go about identifying steering risk? You may have already guessed that the products that they offer, in and of themselves, present steering risk. If a bank has products that vary drastically based on things like interest rates and fees, there may be increased steering risk. That does not mean that a bank cannot charge different interest rates for the same product based on a customer's creditworthiness. That's pricing based on risk which we will get into in a later chapter.

If banks have different product options,
referral channels, or add-on products,
they may have increased steering risk.

Another major indicator for steering risk is how loan officers are paid. Going back to our credit life example, we can see that when a loan officer is incentivized based on the products that they sell, they will often try and maximize their pay by getting customers into loan products that make them more money. The problem with this method is that oftentimes it's certain prohibited basis group applicants that are disproportionately sold higher cost products.

The federal government did pass a law that prohibits loan officer pay to be based on interest rates, fees, and other criteria like loan terms. However, that law only covers home mortgage loans. This leaves out many other consumer-purpose loans such as car loans, recreational vehicles, credit cards, or simple unsecured loans. You can even see lender compensation risk in areas like small business or farm lending. This doesn't mean that a bank cannot pay their lenders for doing a good job and selling products. What it does mean is that a bank should not consider certain terms of a loan when they are deciding on compensation.

If a lender knows they will make more money if they charge a higher interest rate, what do you think they would do? What would you do in that same situation?

Building Prevention into the Steering Process

The good thing about steering risk is that with good policies, procedures, and training, it's a risk that can easily be reduced and sometimes eliminated. If an institution chooses to offer different cost loan products, utilize referral channels, or sell add-on products, they will just need to do more monitoring and testing. A bank needs to have some good procedures in place to spell out how an applicant qualifies for a certain loan product. But just as importantly, they need to follow that guidance consistently. If you need a 720-credit score to get Loan Product A, then require the applicant to actually have a 720-credit score. The problem is lenders often like to stretch that limit and approve someone for Loan Product A with a 700-credit score.

Banks also need to think about loan officer pay to eliminate these risks. The strongest banks I have seen that eliminate this risk make sure they don't pay any lenders based on the terms and conditions of a loan. Add-on products are a bit tougher to have fair compensation but still incentivize lenders to sell the products. If you pay a lender a small bonus to sell credit life insurance, they are more likely to try and sell it. If they know they won't get paid any more and selling a credit life policy only creates more work for them, they are likely to sell less. Bank executives have to balance the risk with the benefits and decide if they want to offer these products and the best way to pay their people to sell them.

Finally, simple monitoring by compliance and audit staff can help identify trends. In our example, we simply asked for a list of credit life policies sold in the year. When we analyzed them and realized they were nearly all to Native American borrowers, potential risk was not hard to find.

Chapter Takeaways

- Know what product options your bank has and how they could increase risk.
- Develop simple procedures to help guide lenders on choosing product options.
- Do periodic monitoring to ensure customers are not placed into higher-cost products on a prohibited basis characteristic.
- Train lenders on your procedures.

The Details

The most common risk I see for steering, outside of the add-on products we discussed, is the rate at which female and minority applicants are being placed into government guaranteed loans. We see this the most in mortgage lending.

Government guaranteed loans are a good thing. As a young 20-something military veteran, I was able to buy my first home using a VA loan with no money down. It allowed me to be able to buy a home years earlier than I would have otherwise been able to. But that VA loan cost thousands in fees, so it was a much higher cost product.

We often see lenders get minority and female applicants into these government guaranteed loans at much higher rates than white and male applicants. The problem is that those applicants that are getting placed into the higher cost government guaranteed loans actually qualified for much lower cost traditional financing.

Ensure you train your loan staff on this very easy to spot risk. Make sure they are getting customers into the best product they qualify for that meets their needs. Finally, monitor your data. There are some great fair lending software programs out there that will do all of the hard work for you. Software shows you how often applicants are put into higher risk products. This makes it easy to see if your institution is doing this process fairly.

CHAPTER SIX

Underwriting Risk

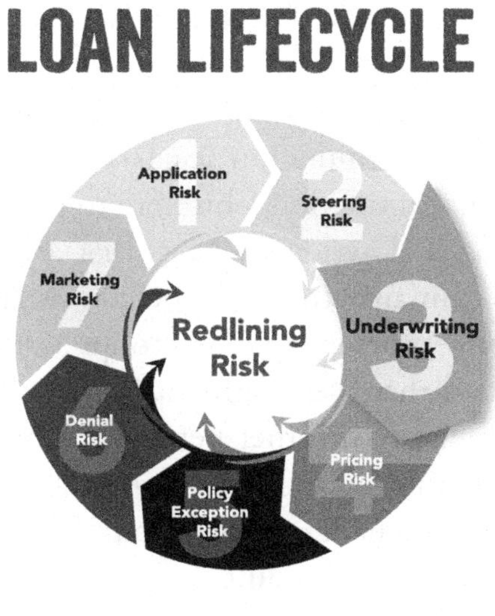

Imagine you are in your local bank branch applying for a loan. The lender has taken your application, and you know what loan product you are going to apply for. Someone at the bank now has to make a loan decision. This is where the approval or denial decision is made. You may be thinking that this is a critical part of the loan lifecycle, and you would be absolutely correct. The process of reviewing your credit score, your ability to make loan payments, and how likely you are to pay back the loan is called underwriting.

Defining Discrimination in Lending

Discrimination is very common in the underwriting process, but is discrimination legal? I want to stretch the definition of discrimination a bit here to prove a point. The Merriam-Webster Dictionary says that discrimination is the practice of unfairly treating a person or group of people differently from other people or groups. Other definitions of the word add that the treatment is typically on the basis of race, sex, religion, or other personal characteristics. Let's simplify the definition and call it *treating people differently*. I'm not trying to change what discrimination means; I'm only trying to illustrate a point.

Go back and look at our original quiz question. True or false – a bank can legally discriminate against a loan applicant. Based on treating people differently, it's absolutely true. When a bank turns down a loan applicant because they have a low credit score, that is discrimination. When an applicant gets turned down because they don't have enough money to repay the loan, that is discrimination. When an applicant is denied because they want more money than the value of the collateral securing the loan, that is discrimination.

However, we need to point out that these are considered legal forms of discrimination. That's basically what underwriting is. Lenders make consistent and fair loan decisions based on legal factors. A bank will not stay in business very long if it doesn't. It's simply unwise to lend money to people with a proven track record of not paying it back. Banks can and should discriminate against applicants who historically either don't pay their bills or cannot afford the loan payments.

I know what you're thinking – I tricked you with that question. Yes and no. You can treat applicants differently in the loan decision. But there are **legal** and **illegal** pieces of criteria you can use to make those decisions. So, when is it illegal to discriminate against a loan applicant? You may have already guessed it by this point.

When loan decisions are made based on
one or more of the prohibited bases,
illegal discrimination has taken place.

You can deny a loan applicant because they have a 400-credit score. You cannot deny a loan applicant because of their race, color, religion, sex, national origin, or any other of the bases under the fair lending laws and regulations. That's why having strong underwriting procedures in place is so important because it ensures that banks are discriminating legally (through underwriting) and not illegally (on a prohibited basis).

How to Set Up a Strong Underwriting Program

You may be asking how would you set up a lending program to ensure that loan decisions are made based on fair and legal criteria? The answer is fairly simple, but it's not as easy to actually implement as one might think. The first and best way to prevent discrimination in the loan underwriting process is to give clear guidance to those people making the loan decision. This is often in the form of a loan policy, but larger banks likely have separate underwriting procedures. Each underwriting factor should be laid out so that every loan officer will consider the same facts and treat customers the same way. The best procedures leave no room for error. Every bank will have their own criteria for making loan decisions. That means that a loan officer needs to learn their own bank's procedures.

There is a good way to test if a bank has strong underwriting procedures in place. This is more of a theory, but the concept teaches us a valuable lesson even if we won't test this in practice. The theory goes like this: If a bank has strong and well-laid out underwriting criteria, they should be able to take any trained loan officer from any bank in the country and give them that criteria. Without that lender asking any questions, just by using those procedures, that lender should be able to come up with the exact same loan decision as any other lender would. It's that simple. Based on my experience, many banks don't come anywhere close to that standard.

I've reviewed program after program where the underwriting guidance is unclear or not at all defined.

Let me use my favorite piece of underwriting criteria that so many banks try and use, but it's pretty horrible every time. It's so bad, I think of it as a curse word in the compliance industry. In fact, I'm going out on a limb and declaring this a swear word in banking: "good customer." I apologize for my foul language, but I had to get it out there.

Too many times an applicant doesn't meet one or more of the standards to get a loan, but they get approved because "they are a good customer." Loan officers love writing that in the loan file. That's great and all, and congratulations for making a loan, but what on earth does being a "good customer" mean? Therein lies the problem. It is so vague that it can mean just about anything, and often does. One lender may think that a good customer is someone who also has a checking account at the bank. Another lender may interpret it as the customer hasn't been late on a loan payment in the past year. The lender in the next office over may think that means no late payments in the past two years. You see the problem here?

Vague underwriting criteria is what gets banks into trouble, and when you don't clearly spell it out for lenders, they make their own interpretations.

Then comes the discrimination because they don't do it fairly and consistently. They are guessing. Most people don't like to guess at how to do their jobs.

The second way to build strength in an underwriting program is to properly train loan staff. There are written and unwritten procedures for pretty much every job in every industry. Some procedures are more critical than others. For example, if you are doing heart surgery, it would be a bad idea to skip steps in the process. Whether you're a stickler for the rules or a rebel that breaks them all, I think we'd all like for our heart surgeon to not be a rule breaker. For banks, spending the time to train loan staff on how to follow procedures can be just as critical as having the procedures themselves.

I've seen too many good procedures in place to only learn through testing that they are never followed. Sometimes it's as simple as training.

The third way to build strength in an underwriting program is through monitoring. Doing simple reviews of loan files is a quick and effective way to ensure that your bank's loan staff are following the great procedures you wrote and are properly trained on how to use them. This doesn't have to be some extravagant process. Simply opening a loan file and determining whether or not loan personnel followed procedures is all it takes. This also acts as a deterrent to lenders because if they know their loan files will be reviewed, they may be less likely to stray away from policy.

The fourth way to build strength in an underwriting program is to follow procedures. Wait, what? We already said that. Well, we did, but there's another point I want to expand upon. It's not that loan officers are not following procedures, it's that they are making exceptions to those procedures. Let's use an example. Let's say a young white male wants to buy a car, but the bank has set the minimum credit score at 650. His credit score happens to be 645. He has plenty of money to pay the loan back along with his other bills, and he is even putting 20 percent as a down payment. Should he be denied for this loan because his credit score is five points below the minimum?

This is where most institutions struggle with fair lending.

Having strong and well-defined procedures decreases fair lending risk. If you always follow procedures every single time, and the loan criteria you are making decisions on are normal underwriting criteria (legal discrimination), it's much less likely you will make a mistake. This is not the world that we live in. Not everybody fits into a box.

Loan officers want to go out of their way to make loans. But every time they make an exception to loan policy, they add a little bit more fair lending risk.

A major question here is when lenders are approving a loan outside of policy, are they doing it consistently? Would a minority applicant in that same situation also get approved? If they don't, there is a problem. The key to underwriting is consistency, and the more loan policy is followed, the less risk there is.

Underwriting Program Options

There are a few different ways that a bank can set up an underwriting program. The size of the bank and their resources usually determine how sophisticated an underwriting program will be. The simplest underwriting program is to have the loan officer underwrite the loan and make the decision. We see this most often in smaller banks. This can be a quick, cheap, and effective method to make loans and serve customers. It also has a higher level of risk because a lot of different people are making loan decisions.

The second way banks can set up an underwriting program is to establish an underwriting department. With this setup, a small group of highly trained individuals will make all loan decisions. As a bank grows and has more lenders and branches, the loan decision process is often taken away from loan officers. The loan officer will take the application and collect all of the information and then forward the application to the underwriting team. Underwriters will then make the decision and communicate that back to the loan officer.

This is a great way to reduce fair lending risk because now only a few people are responsible for loan decisions.

This is also a much more controlled environment. It takes some of the human element out of the loan decision. What I mean by that is lenders often develop personal relationships with their customers. Especially in small towns, customers and lenders work together for years. Because of that, they may be more willing to overlook unfavorable factors such as the fact that a customer doesn't pay back their loans. I know that sounds silly, but it happens all of the time. If you have ever lived or banked in a small town, you know what I mean.

An underwriter is further removed from the personal relationship and can just focus on the facts. This reduces the chances of making bad decisions and exceptions to policy, thus reducing risk. This method is a bit slower to get a loan decision as it adds steps to the process. It's also more costly because a bank now has to pay more people to make the loan decision instead of just the loan officer.

The third underwriting option is an automated program making loan decisions. You will see this setup in the largest banks. In this program, a person rarely ever makes a loan decision. All of the underwriting factors are written into a software program. The loan officer will input all of a customer's criteria, and the software will make a decision. This method is very inflexible, but it's one of the best ways to reduce underwriting risk.

Imagine a bank that has 500 or even 1,000 loan officers. If every one of those loan officers was allowed to make loan decisions, you could have up to 1,000 different ways of making a loan. Automated software eliminates that risk, but it's also harder to approve a customer that doesn't fit perfectly into the box. It's quicker, less risky, but the most inflexible. The largest banks simply don't want to take on the risk and are pretty much forced to use this method. Due to the large scale of loans, it's really the only way for them to control risk.

The last common underwriting program option is a hybrid model. This type of model has some manual and some automated elements to it. For example, a lender may enter all of the data into an automated underwriting software, but they may have the authority to override decisions the software makes. This method can help reduce risk by automating the process while still giving some flexibility in the loan decision process.

Underwriting Criteria – What do Banks Care About?

Let's talk about the facts that someone will consider in making the loan decision or the actual underwriting criteria. What factors does a typical bank consider? In other words, what does the bank care about when they are deciding whether or not they are going to make you a loan? These are the underwriting factors. This list can get quite long, but let's cover some common ones that most banks will use.

Debt-to-income (DTI) Ratio: The DTI ratio is pretty simple. You take all of your monthly debt payments and divide that amount by your monthly income. That ratio is a way to determine if somebody has enough money to pay back the loan. For most home mortgage loans, banks do not want to see that ratio go over 43%. A lower DTI ratio means that a customer has plenty of extra money each month to pay their bills. These customers have significantly less risk because they have not overextended themselves. If you have a high DTI ratio and money gets tight, you have little cash left over to pay your bills.

Loan-to-value (LTV) Ratio: The LTV ratio is calculated whenever a piece of collateral is used to secure the loan. For example, if someone wants to buy a car that is worth $10,000, and they are borrowing $10,000, they have a LTV of 100% (10,000/10,000 = 1 or 100%). Let's change it up and say that same customer is willing to put $3,000 of their own money towards the car. That means the loan amount is now $7,000, but the value is still $10,000. In this case, the LTV would be 70% (7,000/10,000 = 0.7 or 70%).

This ratio is important because the lower the LTV, the less risk of loss to the bank. If a bank has to repossess that car, and they can only sell it for $8,000, they would lose $2,000 when the LTV is 100%. However, in the second example, they would get all of their money back because the loan amount was only $7,000. The lower the LTV, the less risk for the bank.

You may have heard the term that somebody is "underwater" on a loan. What that simply means is their LTV is greater than 100%. The loan amount is higher than the value of the collateral. This was common in the housing crisis from 2007-2009 because customers borrowed money close to what their home was worth, meaning their LTV ratios were near or sometimes over 100%. Nobody seemed to care because housing prices usually just keep climbing up and up, making their LTV ratio go down – until they didn't. Prices can't skyrocket forever. Eventually, the bubble burst, housing prices stopped going up, and the market crashed. Home values went way down, making LTV ratios go way up. Before we knew it, most people owed (**Loan**-to-value) more than their house was worth (loan-to-**Value**), so their LTV was greater than 100%. That's a bad position for a customer and even worse for the bank.

Credit Score: This is one of the easiest and most common methods used to determine if someone has a history of repaying debt on time. A bank reports your repayment behavior to credit bureaus, and those credit bureaus will analyze that (along with other factors) to come up with a three-digit score. The higher your score, the less risk you pose to a bank when they lend you money. Banks then pay the credit bureaus to see your score so that they can help make the decision to approve or deny your loan application.

Age of Collateral: This one is the most critical criterion for collateral with a title like a car, boat, recreational vehicle, or anything else fun in life to drive. For example, the age of a car is a critical piece of information because as a car gets older, the value goes down significantly. We all know that a new car loses a good chunk of value the moment it is driven off the lot. Taking that into consideration, if someone borrows 100 percent of the loan amount, they could possibly have an LTV over 100 percent on that new car the moment they drive away. The other main factor is the useful life of the car.

If most cars only last 10 years, and the car you want to buy is already 7 years old, does it make sense to give you a 5-year timeframe to repay the loan? Age of collateral is a big factor in determining how long you will get to repay a loan.

Other criteria: There are additional criteria that lenders typically use. Things like how long an applicant has been in their current job is important. If somebody is always switching jobs, they carry more risk, as they might not always have a steady income to pay back the loan. The same with how long someone has been in their home or lived in the local area. People with a stable living situation carry less risk for repayment.

As I mentioned earlier, any underwriting criteria a lender uses should be very well-defined. You should be able take a lender from any bank and put them in any other bank with only the underwriting criteria provided. They should be able to follow that guidance and make the same decision as any other lender without further assistance. If an underwriting program is spelled out that well, a bank has greatly reduced their risk in this area.

Building Prevention Into The Underwriting Process

We've covered that pretty heavily. A bank's underwriting program should match the size and complexity of the bank. A bank with 500 branches shouldn't have poorly defined guidance and let every lender make their own decisions. The program has to make sense for the size of the bank.

Criteria and guidance need to be well defined. Saying someone needs to be a "good customer" doesn't cut it. What makes them a good customer; a good credit score? What is that score? Banks need to define it. If lenders are left to guess on how to do their job, some are going to guess wrong. Nobody wants to make mistakes. Give loan officers the tools to do their job the right way.

Finally, monitoring and auditing are effective tools to identify and lower risk in this area. Simple file reviews to see if lenders are following underwriting guidelines and procedures is an easy way to test a program. There are software programs that also help banks ensure consistent loan decisions. Software can easily automate the process and provide useful data instantly. That won't fix issues that have happened, so it's a reactive measure, but it can help identify weaknesses and prevent further issues if used effectively.

Underwriting doesn't need to be complicated. It just needs to be clearly defined and consistently followed.

Chapter Takeaways

- Establish clearly defined underwriting criteria.
- Minimize exceptions to policy.
- Set up an underwriting program that makes sense for the size and complexity of the bank.
- Train lenders on the right way to make a loan.

The Details

If you are a compliance officer, you need to be digging deep into your bank's underwriting criteria. You should be looking at all criterion objectively to decide if there is anyway someone could interpret it differently. If there is any way that someone could read a loan decision factor differently than intended, it's not good enough.

Depending on the size of your bank, software is a great way to test your process. You can build in all of your underwriting criterion and see if lenders are making consistent and fair loan decisions. When red flags pop up, you need to dig in and find out what is going on.

You can easily build in simple file reviews as part of your compliance management system. Grab a handful of files at the end of each month and just see if lenders are following policy. Always choose different lenders, branches, and markets for your reviews. It's not hard to recreate a loan decision and see if policy was followed. If there was an exception to policy, check your exception log to see if it was approved and tracked.

Your management team will need to take the lead in setting the tone of policy compliance at your bank. If management likes "winging it" when making loan decisions and doesn't see an issue with going outside of policy, it's your job to explain the risk to them.

As compliance and audit professionals, it's our job to identify risk. It's management's job to control it.

CHAPTER SEVEN

Pricing Risk

LOAN LIFECYCLE

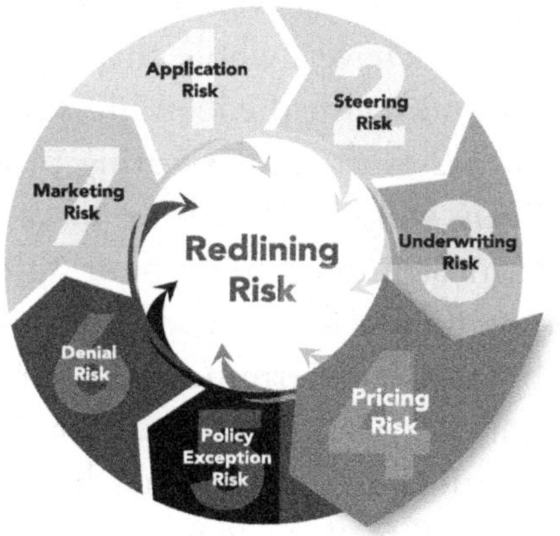

Buying a home is one of the single biggest purchases most people will ever make. The price of the home is significant, but that's only part of the cost. When you get a home loan, you of course pay interest on that money for upwards of 30 years. Home loans are often refinanced, but it's not uncommon for people to make house payments for decades of their lives. The interest that you pay for all of those years can equate to hundreds of thousands of dollars, depending on what interest rate you get.

What if you were to get a higher rate, simply because of the color of your skin? What if you paid a higher rate because your home was located in a certain part of town? I'm sure you would like to believe that all loan officers have a pre-approved loan pricing guideline that ensures consistent and fair pricing to everyone. Well, there's a reason why I tell this story and why we have a whole chapter on loan pricing.

Let's go back and revisit the loan lifecycle of risks. Once a loan applicant passes the underwriting process and is approved, they likely will be offered the loan. The next step, and one of the most important, is figuring out how much that loan is going to cost the borrower. This is a critical step for the bank because it determines how much revenue the loan will bring in. It's also very critical for the borrower because, as we mentioned, it determines how much you will have to pay over the life of the loan.

Loan pricing is one of the simplest steps of the loan lifecycle, but it can get complicated and out-of-control very quickly.

What is Loan Pricing?

There are a few parts to the pricing process that I want to cover first. The most obvious piece that likely comes to your mind is the interest rate. When you borrow money from a bank, you pay the money back over time with interest. The lower the interest rate, the less that you will have to pay back on top of what you borrowed (the principle). That's not groundbreaking news by any means. But the interest rate is not the only cost of a loan. Fees can often make up a large part of the loan cost. Most traditional lending institutions have smaller fees for consumer loans. They make most of their money off of the interest rate. However, some lenders, like payday lenders and vehicle title lenders, charge much higher fees.

A $50 fee on a $10,000 loan doesn't seem like a lot, and generally, it's reasonable. But a $50 fee on a $250 loan can be very significant. There are other laws and regulations that lenders must follow that will spread out those fees over an annual basis to help applicants see just how much those fees impact a loan. You may have seen loan documents that state your interest rate, but it also states an Annual Percentage Rate, or APR.

The APR is the true rate you pay when you spread out loan fees over the life of the loan.

I won't go into more details than that other than to say when you are shopping for a loan, make sure you compare APRs, not just the interest rate. This will help ensure you don't underestimate the fees when it comes to loans. They can add up quick!

The loan term is another part of the pricing process that most people don't think about. What do I mean by loan term? The loan term is the amount of time that a customer has to pay back a loan. For example, it is common to have a 60-month loan term on a car. That means a customer has five years (60 months) of monthly payments to pay back the amount borrowed.

Loan terms are usually often closely tied to the age of the collateral, in this case a car.

We talked about this more in the underwriting chapter. A bank will often give six or seven years to pay back a large loan on a brand-new car. They know that car will still have some value left over at the end of the term, so they give you more time to pay it off. This helps lower the payments for the borrower into something more affordable and manageable.

However, a bank likely will not give you seven years to pay back a car that is 10 years old. At the end of that loan term, that car will be 17 years old, assuming the car still even runs! In those cases, a lender may only give a three-year term. The longer a customer has to pay back a loan, the more risk there is because that's more time for something to go wrong.

How to Build a Fair Pricing Model

How is a bank supposed to ensure that everybody gets priced fairly? First of all, is it fair to give everyone the same interest rate? When you think of this question and answer, it may seem logical to think that everybody should get the same rate. However, it can be a lot more complicated than that. We just talked about the type of car somebody is going to buy. If a customer buys a brand-new car, that collateral will have a lot more value than a 10-year-old car and a much longer useful life span. That, in turn, means there is not as much risk to a lender.

When risk increases, the price increases.

That's called risk-based pricing, and it is a common practice in lending. Risk goes up, price goes up. If you are putting your money at risk, you want to make sure you get paid for that risk. Putting your money in a deposit account at a bank is very low-risk. Your deposits are insured by the FDIC (up to certain limits), so you know that you're getting your money back with interest. The interest is very little, though, because there is no risk.

When you invest in the stock market, the businesses you invest in can fail, and you can lose everything. That's why you make more money in the stock market than depositing your money into a bank account. Risk goes up, price goes up. Using this train of thought, we would expect a lender to price loans differently based on the risk each customer presents.

Another key factor of pricing loans is the likelihood of a bank not getting its money back. Now we are talking about the creditworthiness of the borrower, or the underwriting factors. Thinking back to what we talked about in underwriting; this is where we want to know what somebody's credit score is. The higher your credit score, the more likely you are to pay back a loan. The more likely you are to pay back a loan, the less risk you present, and thus a lower interest rate. It's a pretty simple concept, but it's important.

Developing a Rate Sheet

How does a bank management team make sure that its loan officers are pricing loans fairly and consistently?

One of the easiest ways to control pricing risk is to establish an interest rate sheet.

This is a sample chart, table, or document given to lenders that instructs them what interest rates to charge based on the criteria and characteristics of the borrower and collateral. We commonly see credit scores on interest rate sheets. As somebody's credit score goes down, you will see the interest rate go up. We also commonly see the age of the collateral on an interest rate sheet. As a car gets older, rates go up.

The other piece of information we normally see on the rate sheet is a loan term. We talked about giving customers longer to pay back a loan on a new car than a used car. However, there is a second factor that must be considered when determining how long of a loan term a customer will get. I have already mentioned that: the longer you give someone to pay back a loan, the more risk there is that something will go wrong.

If you want a longer term to pay back your car loan, you can expect to pay a higher interest rate.

A home loan is a bit different than a car loan. First of all, as long as the borrowers take care of the home, the home's value generally goes up. Yes, there are many other factors that can have an impact on a home's change in value, but over time, home values tend to increase. This means the general risk to the bank goes down.

Let's look at it solely from a bank's standpoint. If they have to repossess the collateral and sell it, will they get their money back? We talked about this in underwriting, but there is crossover in pricing too. That concept is the same for car loans as it is for home loans, but cars generally lose value and homes generally increase in value, so the length of the loan terms differ drastically.

The other major factor that affects the loan term length for a home loan is the simple fact that homes are expensive! Most customers cannot pay off a home in five years. It's common to see anywhere from 15 to 30 years to pay off a home loan. Giving someone 360 months (30 years) to pay off a home gets the monthly payments to a level the average consumer can afford.

Now that you have seen the different factors that go into the price of the loan, you can start to paint the picture in your head the amount of risk present in this process. If a bank makes only a few hundred loans a year, there is some risk on whether or not that bank is pricing consistently. If a bank makes thousands or tens of thousands of loans a year, that risk rises significantly. That's a lot more opportunities to discriminate.

Just like with underwriting,
the pricing process can also be automated.

Larger banks have a software program that automatically prices the loan. The lender simply inputs all of the criteria, and the software says what the rate will be. Using this method, you take out the human factor and only consider the legal forms of discrimination – underwriting factors. Most small to medium-sized banks do not have automated software, so they rely on a well-crafted rate sheet and lenders doing their jobs by actually following the rate sheet.

As with underwriting, a bank's process for pricing loans is only useful if loan officers are actually following them. A bank can have the most beautiful and thought-out rate sheet imaginable (if you think rate sheets are beautiful), but if lenders don't use it, it does nothing to lower fair lending risk. I want to talk about two different ends of the spectrum by discussing some real-world examples I've seen in my career.

Real-World Example – Across the Board Pricing

As a bank examiner, I once did a fair lending review where a small bank did not have an interest rate sheet. That is a bit unusual as nearly every institution has a rate sheet these days. So, I asked the bank president why their bank did not have a rate sheet. His response was simple: "Everyone gets the same rate!" He pretty much screamed it at me. Everybody that came to that bank got the same interest rate. He did not want to have any fair lending risk, so he just decided everybody would get the same rate. He was so scared of discrimination and pricing risk that he just eliminated any chance of it completely.

Is it okay to do that? Well, yes. If you give the same rate to every customer, nobody will be treated differently on a prohibited basis. In the end, that's what banks should really be trying to prevent – discrimination in pricing. However, is it wise to give the same interest rate to your best customers with an 800-credit score that you give the worst customers with a 500-credit score?

Banks that choose this method of pricing loans will not be competitive, and they will lose business because of it.

If you have a good credit score and one bank wants to charge you 3% more than another bank, what would you do? You should have strong pricing practices in place, but if you go overboard and have such rigid practices as this, you are going to lose a lot of business. Did this bank president eliminate his pricing risk? Yes. Is he going to pay for that in other ways? Also, yes.

Maybe giving everyone the same rate is not the best way to control pricing risk or to run a lending operation. Let's talk about another bank exam that was on the other end of the pricing spectrum.

Real-World Example – The Wild West of Loan Pricing

I once did an examination for a smaller bank that had a formal interest rate sheet. I call it a rate sheet because they had interest rates written on it, but it was one of the worst rate sheets I've ever seen. It was very broad and provided very poor guidance to loan staff. Honestly, they probably would have been better off without a rate sheet.

This bank offered unsecured loans (as most do). These types of loans carry the most risk because there is no collateral to repossess if the customer stops paying. Because of this, these loans are priced very high to make up for the increased risk.

The way this bank structured their rate sheet was that if a customer's credit score was lower than 660, the lender was supposed to price the loan at 18%. If their credit score was 660 or higher, the lender was supposed to price the loan between 10% to 18%. That was it. That was the rate sheet. Management gave their lenders 8 percent of an interest rate spread to price their loans.

They never monitored the lender's performance and never performed an audit to see if lenders were doing it fairly.

In banking, they use the term basis points when they talk about rates. One one-hundredth of a percent is one basis point, or 0.01. A full percent, or 1%, would then be 100 basis points. Based on my years of doing fair lending audits, I've found that many banks will give lenders the authority to change the rate by 25 basis points, and some will go as high as even 50 or a 100 basis points. Personally, I have a lower risk tolerance, so I think 25 basis points is a lot. This bank gave their lenders 800 basis points of pricing discretion! I will tell you straight up, 800 basis points is a lot of disparity. That was a major red flag.

When I saw this interest rate sheet, I knew this bank had a lot of pricing risk. I also knew right away that I was going to do a pricing review. Now this was a small bank. They only had a single location and three lenders. So, while they have a lot of risk because they gave so much pricing discretion to their lenders, the risk was limited to three people in one location. That was the good news.

All three of the lenders were white male loan officers. Let's call them loan officers A, B and C. Loan Officer A was the president and owner of the bank. Loan officers B and C were vice presidents with no ownership. Since the location of the bank had a very low minority population, we used the prohibited basis of sex for our review. In a nutshell, we wanted to know if lenders were pricing loans to men at similar rates that they were to women.

To conduct the pricing review, we found the average interest rate given to men and compared that to women.

We first looked at all of the lenders combined and found that lenders were giving female borrowers an average rate of more than 2% higher than males, or 200 basis points. That was the next red flag. I then was able to break down the data further by each individual loan officer to see how each lender performed. I wasn't using any fancy software to do this by the way, just a Microsoft Excel spreadsheet and a list of loans.

I found that Loan Officer B's average rate to male borrowers was 7%. No male borrower ever got in the 10% - 18% range that everyone was supposed to be in. In fact, no male ever got over 9%. That means that this lender never priced a single loan within the rate sheet parameters. I then calculated the average rate he gave to female borrowers, and it was also 7%. Everyone got between 5% - 9%, and nobody was in the 10% - 18% range that everyone was supposed to be in.

At first, I noticed that this lender is WAY outside of loan policy, but at least he was pricing fairly and consistently to both men and women.

This is still a major risk since the lender is never following official bank policy, but it's not necessarily a fair lending risk because this prohibited basis category was priced fairly.

I then looked at Loan Officer C. His numbers looked nearly identical to Loan Officer B. The average rate he gave to men was 7%. The average rate he gave to women was also 7%. At that point, I am thinking that they probably have an informal rate of 7%. I've seen this before where a small bank sort of has a "going rate" where they use some internal base rate and price their loans around that rate. Small banks usually can get away with controlling that risk because they have only a few lenders, but this bank had a rate sheet.

If they had a rate sheet, they should be using it.

I knew right away that neither lender was following policy as not a single customer was in the range that all customers were supposed to be in. This is a perfect example of poor guidance (rate sheet with 800 basis points of discretion) that was never followed (both lenders ignored the rate sheet). So far, I did not find issues within these two lenders, at least from a fair lending and consistency standpoint. Then I got to Loan Officer A.

Remember, this gentleman was the president and owner of the bank. The average interest rate he gave to men was also 7%. That's the same average Loan Officers B and C priced to men. However, the average rate Loan Officer A gave to women – 14%! He was charging women double the rate than men for the same loan. What's worse, every single loan made to a woman was priced in the range of 10% - 18%. Basically, what he was doing was holding women to the standard of the interest rate sheet when he himself for men, and all of the other loan officers for every other borrower was pricing around 7%.

He thought he was doing his job by following the rate sheet, but he was only following the rate sheet for one prohibited basis group – women.

The ironic part of this case is that if the bank did not have a rate sheet, he probably would have priced women closer to men, as the other two loan officers did. Since they had a poorly written rate sheet, and he decided to follow it for women only, he discriminated on the prohibited basis of sex.

If you've never been a young, fairly inexperienced federal bank regulator that just discovered rampant pricing discrimination by a wealthy bank president and owner, I can tell you it's quite an eye-opening experience. Fortunately for me, I was farmed out for that assignment to a different area and wasn't the one that had to deal with it. I was able to walk up to the Examiner-in-Charge and basically say, "Hey, the bank president is discriminating against women. Well, my review is done, so I'm going to head home now." Nobody wants to accuse a business owner of discriminating, but that's part of the job. Thankfully, this time it was not my job.

Lessons Learned

This example gives us a couple lessons. A poorly written pricing program can go bad in a hurry. Sometimes as little as 75 basis point disparities between prohibited basis groups (in this case, males and females) can be a major issue. This bank president had 700 basis points of pricing disparity. Even with a small loan sample, that's a significant difference. The other lesson to take away is why it's important to consistency follow procedures.

A rate sheet is a procedure. When it is well defined and consistently followed, risk can nearly disappear.

In this case, it was poorly defined (giving lenders 800 basis point discretion) and inconsistently followed (only one lender used it for only one prohibited basis group), so risk went through the roof.

Building Prevention into the Pricing Process

Several factors should be considered when a bank is building a pricing program. If a bank is small with only a few lenders and branches, the process can be more informal. A bank can rely on a well-defined rate sheet. They can train their lenders to consistently follow it and use simple reviews to verify that fact. As the bank grows, the process is harder to control. At that point, banks may want to look at automating the process and limiting a lender's authority to stray away from the rate sheet. This is where exception risk comes in. Anytime a lender approves a loan at a rate, term, or fee amount outside of the rate sheet, or when they approve a loan for someone who doesn't meet underwriting criteria, a loan exception is made. Every exception increases fair lending risk.

Chapter Takeaways

- Establish strong pricing procedures either through a rate sheet or formal pricing model.
- Larger banks should consider automated pricing procedures.
- Train your lenders on how to properly price loans.
- Track any deviations from the rate sheet and monitor trends for fairness.

The Details

Pricing is one of the biggest risks in the loan lifecycle, but it's also one of the easiest to track. Every time I teach about pricing, I always imagine Oprah. She's shouting out to the audience that "You get a rate, and you get a rate, and everyone gets a rate!" If you aren't familiar with that reference, Oprah once gave out cars to everyone in her audience. Unfortunately, I wasn't there that day.

Anyway, all customers get a rate. Therefore, we can compare them to one another, plug in some prohibited basis group characteristics, and see if lenders are pricing fairly and consistently.

If your bank is a stickler on pricing, and you always follow the rate sheet, you may have very little pricing risk. Many banks don't operate that way. The more pricing discretion your bank gives to your lenders, the more risk you have. That's your biggest issue to deal with.

Having strong policies and procedures in place is the

best way to reduce fair lending risk. It really shuts the door on discrimination if you have a solid model that is built free and clear of discrimination. However, every time lenders go outside of policy, you open up risk a little more, and a little more, until your strong policies and procedures are useless. That's where exception risk comes in, which just so happens to be our next topic.

CHAPTER EIGHT

Policy Exception Risk

Not everybody fits neatly into a box. Some people are better at managing money than others. That's likely someone you know, or maybe you. Some people are much better at paying their bills on time. Some people don't pay their bills at all (We all know some of them.). One person may prioritize having a bigger home, so they will want to borrow as much as possible to buy a house. Some people like to buy lots of fun toys while others prioritize saving. The point is that everyone is unique when it comes to handling and borrowing money.

Banks try and create these boxes. There are underwriting boxes where you have to have a minimum credit score and maximum DTI ratio to get approved. There are also these pricing boxes where if you buy a car that is three years old and want five years to pay it back, you will get exactly this interest rate. Those are policies, and you should know them well by now. But what happens if someone doesn't quite fit into the box? What if someone's credit score is just a bit low, their LTV ratio is a bit high, or they want you to match your quoted rate to the lender down the street? Those are loan policy exceptions, and they bring a whole new level of risk that we have to manage.

Let me be the first to welcome you to the loan policy exception process. Policy exceptions are a lenders best friend and a compliance officer's worst nightmare. This process is one of the most critical in the entire loan life cycle. This is where lenders throw caution to the wind to make a deal and see how it pays off. Risky, but it happens. Every. Single. Day.

Strong policies and procedures are the best way to lower fair lending risk.

I want to repeat that. Strong policies and procedures are the best way to lower fair lending risk. Having good underwriting procedures in place that are consistently followed will ensure that a loan officer makes fair loan decisions to all applicants. Having a strong interest rate sheet or an automated process ensures that people get a fair and consistent rate.

However, the world is a bit more complicated than that. What if my credit score is five points below a bank's minimum requirement? What if a bank down the street is offering a better rate on the loan than your bank is offering? Should your bank lose that loan because it's not willing to come down a little bit on the interest rate? Is that fair to the bank, the lender, or the customer? That depends on who you are trying to treat fairly.

Here's the big question: Should somebody be denied if they don't fit perfectly into all of the boxes?

Loan exceptions can be viewed as a positive. It's going out of your way to ensure that customers get the money they need to buy a car, build a house, go to college, or pay bills. When a bank makes an exception, they are also bringing in additional business. Every business (banks included) needs customers. Only so many of those customers are going meet all of your criteria to get a loan. If a bank expands those criteria just a bit, there are more opportunities to lend money. When does the loan policy exception process become a fair lending issue?

Policy exceptions become an issue when those exceptions are no longer made on a fair and consistent basis but rather on a prohibited basis.

What Exceptions Look Like

There are many chances to make an exception in the loan process. Let's talk about a couple of the most common. The first area to make exceptions is in the underwriting process. You can take any one of the underwriting criteria we discussed, and if you approve a loan for a customer that does not meet those criteria, an exception is made. "Sir, you need a 625-credit score for this loan. Even though your credit score is only 618, we are going to approve you." That's how loan exceptions are born.

Pricing is the other most common area for potential exceptions. If you get an interest rate that is different than what's on the rate sheet, an exception is made. This one happens all of the time. "Such and such bank down the street is offering 4 percent for this loan. If you can match that, I will get the loan here." This happens daily across the country. It's not just other banks that your bank has to worry about – it's any other company that lends money. This includes credit unions, specialty lenders, and especially auto finance companies.

"The dealership is offering me 0% for 72 months on this car." How can a bank compete with 0% interest? What that customer likely doesn't realize is that they added thousands on to the cost of the car. That "dealer finance company" you are getting your loan through is not giving you free money for 6 years, but that's another topic for another day.

Loan Term Exception

The interest rate is not the only time we see exceptions in the pricing process. If you give somebody a longer loan term than what is on the rate sheet, that is also an exception. This one is very common, but most people don't think of it as a policy exception. Here's how it works. Let's say a customer qualifies for a 48-month repayment term on a car they want to buy. The customer looks at what the payments will be and realizes it's a little bit higher than they are comfortable paying each month. What does the lender do? They give the customer 60 months to repay the loan but at the 48-month interest rate. There could be two possible exceptions here.

Remember how we said the longer a bank allows a customer to pay back a loan, the higher the risk? Banks tend to only give longer loan terms to the most qualified buyers. If a car buyer only qualifies for a 48-month loan, but a lender gives them 60 months, they potentially made an underwriting exception. If they give them the 48-month interest rate, they also made a pricing exception. Shorter term loans (48 months) typically have lower rates than longer term loans (60 months) because they carry less risk. We possibly just had two loan policy exceptions in one decision to give another year to pay back the loan.

Fee Exceptions

Nearly all customers are price-sensitive. Everybody wants to get the best price. There is nothing wrong with that. However, most consumers always negotiate on the interest rate. So, most of the exceptions in the pricing process are on rates. But, there is another big part of loan pricing that most people forget about. Fees!

If you have a $200 origination fee, and a bank waives that fee, that is also an exception.

Some banks (usually smaller banks) just don't bother charging fees. They simply make their money on the interest rate. Others like to hike up their fees and give you a lower rate. Every consumer needs to watch out for this. You think you're getting a good deal on a 2% loan, but you're paying these fees that you never think about. In the end, you could be paying the same or more than if you had lower fees and a higher interest rate.

The other kicker with fees is those are generally non-refundable. That means you pay these big fees up front and never get them back. If you pay off your loan early, the bank already got its money. If you decide instead to pay lower fees and a higher rate, the bank doesn't make as much if you pay off the loan early. I may be digressing a bit, but it's an important thing to think about when getting a loan. Banks waiving fees are a lot less common of an exception because most borrowers never even think to ask. All everyone cares about is the rate.

Reducing Policy Exception Risk

Let's go back to a common theme in this book. Strong policies and procedures are the best way to reduce fair lending risk. A bank's policies and procedures are their underwriting criteria, checklists, interest rate sheets, software, and any other processes they use to make the loan decision. Consistently following procedures reduces risk. Every time a banker goes outside of policy and procedures, risk goes up a little bit. If they go outside of procedures often, risk goes up much higher.

Pretty soon, a lender just stops following rate sheets all together and ends up charging women twice as much than men to get the same loan.

How do we go out of our way to make loans exceptions and match competition but still control fair lending risk? The first thing a bank can do is build exception within their policy. Banks want to have multiple relationships with their customers. They don't want to just make someone a car loan and that's it. They also want to make them a home loan, have their checking and saving accounts, give them a credit card, lend them money for college, help them buy a boat, and help with retirement planning. Banks want to handle all of your finances. It's what they are good at, so offering all of these products and services makes sense.

Banks can reduce cost and increase profits by fully taking care of one customer (have all of your business) as opposed to partially taking care of multiple customers (only have a loan or deposit account from many different people). This is relationship banking, and it's done through cross selling. When taken to the extreme, this can go very wrong in a hurry. There is a very public case of one of the largest banks on the planet opening up fake accounts for customers to build those "relationships." I don't want to name names, but I'll just say the bank's name rhymes with Wells Fargo. Again, I digress.

Build Exceptions Into Policy

Having multiple relationships with a bank is not necessarily a bad thing. In fact, banks often build exceptions into their loan process around those relationships that benefit you. For example, they may give you a lower interest rate on your car loan if you also have a checking account with them. I often see lower interest rates for setting up automatic payments on a loan. I've seen discounts on rates when you have your paycheck direct deposited in your checking account at the same bank. Sometimes there will be discounts if you have multiple loans or if you have multiple overall relationships. All of those are acceptable and a great way to reduce risk while still being flexible and meeting the customer's needs.

When those types of exceptions are built within the program, it reduces the risk, as long as they are always given to customers every time they qualify. Obviously, if this process is automated in the software, the computer handles it. If a bank employee has to manually give those discounts, errors can happen, and customers may not get the discounts they earned.

When a loan officer is supposed to give a customer a rate discount (by policy) and they forget, technically that is now a policy exception.

You can see how attention to detail matters.

Putting Controls in Place

The next step to reducing exception risk is by controlling the exception process itself. One person should not be allowed to make exceptions whenever they feel like it. If a lender can go outside of loan policy without approval, they are essentially making up their own policy. Having an approval authority for exceptions above the loan officer level is a great way to help control the risk. This ensures that an institution doesn't have lenders getting out of hand, going way outside of policy, or making exceptions all of the time. It also helps make sure exceptions are made fairly and consistently, no matter what lender you go to. Having that control and oversight across many lenders and branches helps reduce risk, but it does not eliminate it.

Here's an important thought that I've seen too many loan officers lose sight of. Exceptions should be just that – an exception.

If loan officers are making exceptions more than 50% of the time, they are no longer exceptions. That's their new operating normal.

Real-World Example

I was conducting a fair lending audit for a client, and I was doing an interview with one of the bank's loan officers. I asked the loan officer how often he felt he made exceptions to policy. He nervously laughed and then said that he makes exceptions 80% - 90% of the time! It was almost like he was proud of it. He was basically never following loan policy and obviously had no idea the amount of risk he was bringing into the bank.

Track and Monitor Exceptions

A third way to lower risk in this area is to track exceptions. Every time a loan officer makes an exception to policy, that exception should be recorded and tracked. Any relevant details should be recorded along with the policy exception. Having an exception tracking log serves a couple purposes. Number one, it lets the loan officers know that they are being monitored and acknowledges that loan exceptions have additional risk. Number two, it can be used for later tracking if a loan goes into default. When a loan goes bad and has to be written off, management can see if a loan exception was made. That helps determine whether or not the loan should have been made in the first place.

Let me state the obvious here – if a loan exception is required (especially for underwriting), the institution is making a loan to someone that doesn't normally qualify. In other words, they are taking on additional risk – so the risk of the loan going bad is higher. Tracking exceptions for fairness is the point I wanted to make, but it also serves other purposes.

Analyze Exceptions

Another benefit of tracking loan exceptions brings us to our fourth way of lowering risk and a key point of why banks should track exceptions at all – to do an analysis. It is amazing that there are so many banks out there that don't track exceptions at all. I figured that about half of the banks I've audited don't track anything for exceptions. I don't ever recommend this practice, and examiners nearly always criticize it in my experience. However, most banks that do track exceptions don't do anything with them! They don't ever do anything in the way of analyzing the data they spent all of that time gathering.

Writing down on a piece of paper that a loan exception was made has absolutely no benefit unless you're going to take the additional step and analyze to find out if you're making exceptions fairly.

That's the key, and that's the whole point of tracking exceptions. As I've helped banks analyze their data, I found some that always make exceptions for men and not women. I've found that they always make exceptions for white borrowers and not black borrowers. I find that 25% of their communities are made up of Hispanic borrowers, but Hispanic borrowers only got 5% of the exceptions. The whole point of tracking exceptions is to see if a bank is making exceptions fairly and consistently or if those exceptions are made on a prohibited basis.

The size of a bank and the number of loans they make will determine how often they should do an analysis of loan exceptions. Small banks may only need to review exceptions once a year. I've seen banks that track all exceptions, and they literally only have 10 to 20 policy exceptions in a whole year. It's pretty easy to see if they are being done fairly and consistently. Larger banks may be looking at them quarterly. They have way too many exceptions to wait until the end of the year to find potential negative trends.

The largest banks likely will be doing an analysis monthly or just do it on-going. For larger banks, they also will want to look at trends. So, every quarter or every month when they are looking at new data, they should be going back the past 12 months and see how their exceptions are trending. Having a rolling 12 months of data can help alert management that exceptions are trending one way or another.

How to Do an Exceptions Analysis

What does a good exceptions analysis look like? To answer that, we just need to answer why we are doing an exceptions analysis.

The reason why you want to look at exceptions is to make sure that they are given on a fair and consistent basis and not on a prohibited basis.

There are a couple of different things a bank should be doing. First, they need to collect relevant data to be able to perform a useful analysis. For home loans, it's much easier. The ECOA requires banks to collect certain data about applicants like their race, ethnicity, sex, marital status, and age. With a little work, a bank can add that information to their exceptions tracking log and look to see if they are giving exceptions fairly.

There are also tools out there that help banks determine certain prohibited basis group characteristics that will allow for a deeper analysis. The analysis should fit the risk profile, size, and complexity of the bank. As I mentioned already, I've seen small banks that make only a few exceptions during the year. That exceptions analysis may take a whole five minutes.

Larger banks may make dozens or hundreds of exceptions a day. That is going to take a lot more time and resources to analyze that data. There are software programs out there that can automatically track and help banks monitor this process. The bigger the bank, the more likely you will need to spend the money and get the automated help.

I want to point out that the size of a bank isn't the biggest indicator of risk for policy exceptions. If a bank has automated software that does all of the underwriting and loan pricing, and no exceptions are allowed, there's no analysis to do. If a bank doesn't allow exceptions, yes, they won't make as many loans, but they won't have the risk either. Some banks draw a hard line in the sand and risk losing business to keep their fair lending risk down. There's nothing wrong with that. All bank executives need to make that risk management decision on how they want to run their bank.

In the end, all that we are trying to figure out is are exceptions being made fairly and consistently.

If a bank's lenders always follow loan policy, there is very little risk. If a bank allows for exceptions to loan policy but they monitor and analyze those exceptions, there is risk, but it's at least better controlled. If a bank allows for exceptions and they never track and monitor, they have the most risk because they really have no idea if their program is fair.

How Much Risk is too Much?

I will tell you that most banks allow for exceptions. Banking is too competitive of an environment to have inflexible underwriting and pricing standards. The big question then is what is an acceptable rate of exceptions? The answer is that there is no magic number or ratio. Every bank and management team has its own internal risk level. One manager may feel that exceptions on more than 10% of loans is too much risk while another manager may feel that exceptions 40% of the time is okay. The point is, every bank should have their own standards and be monitoring to ensure they are within those set standards.

Too many banks have no idea what their loan staff are doing and how much risk they are taking on.

Building Prevention into the Exception Process

First of all, consider adding exceptions into loan policy. This is the fairest and easiest way to control the process. If you're willing to give rate breaks for having other accounts, build that right into the pricing model.

Put an approval process in place for exceptions. Banks that allow any lender to make exceptions without prior approval, by far, carry the highest risk. When there is a formal approval process in place, they help ensure that all lenders are making exceptions the same. Adding layers to the exception approval process also helps control risk across different branches and departments. It also can act as a deterrent to lenders asking for exceptions if they know they need to get it approved.

Put a tracking program in place. Whenever an exception is made, it needs to be recorded on an exception log. For smaller banks, this is often a manual process. That means that either the lender themselves will have to put it on the log or the person approving the exception will. For larger banks, this can be automated. Either way, make sure all exceptions are recorded.

Do a periodic analysis of those exceptions. How complicated and how often this analysis gets depends on how big the bank is and how many exceptions they make. Another good metric is how often exceptions are being made.

If lenders are showing up on the tracking log all of the time and have a high rate of exceptions, training may be in order.

Remember: exceptions can be a good thing, but they have to be done fairly. In the end, that's the whole point of all of this – treating all people fairly and not on a prohibited basis. By putting these processes in place, every bank can help reduce fair lending risk in this vital part of the loan life cycle.

Chapter Takeaways

- Build exceptions into policy whenever possible.
- Require secondary approval by a higher lending authority.
- Track and monitor all exceptions.
- Perform a periodic analysis to ensure they are done fairly and consistently.
- Set standards and expectations for your loan staff on what is and what is not acceptable.

The Details

I mentioned earlier that loan policy exceptions are a lender's best friend because they allow them to make more loans. However, they are a compliance officer's worst enemy. Every exception adds risk, and it's our job to find that risk.

I've sat in front of many bank executives and loan administrative professionals and have asked what is an acceptable rate of exceptions for their lender to have? Not once yet have I gotten an immediate response. Yes, they will take some time and think about it, but it's always an afterthought. Does your bank set those standards?

Personally, I'm a bit risk averse when it comes to high rates of exceptions. I like to see low exception rates. It greatly controls risk and makes my job and life much easier. Talk with your management teams and challenge them to come up with standards. Maybe you want to keep exceptions to less than 20% of loans. Great! Have that standard and measure your lenders against it.

Not sure what to do for an analysis? Just start somewhere! Find out the rate of exceptions to men and women on the year. Find the rate of exceptions to Hispanic borrowers. Does that line up with the rate of loans, or how about your assessment area population demographics? If 30% of your loans went to Hispanic borrowers, but they only got 4% of all exceptions, that's a red flag. Start somewhere and then build upon it.

With all reviews you do, write a report, even a brief one, and send that up the management chain, preferably to the Board. Compliance examiners love reading Board minutes that contain compliance discussions. Why? Because they don't see it often, and it shows your Board is involved and cares about compliance and fair lending.

CHAPTER NINE

Denial Risk

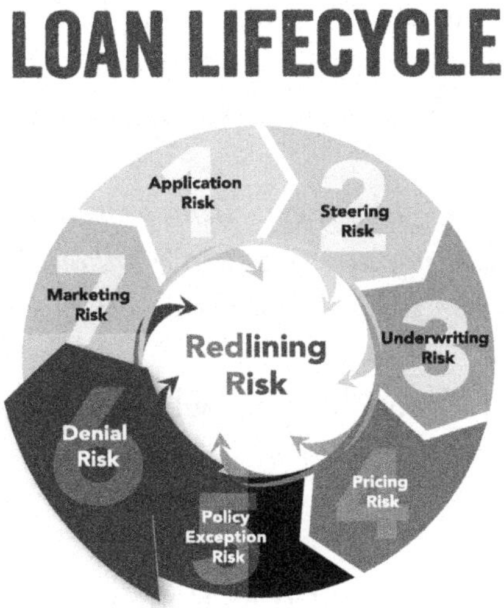

I think back to my childhood days and playing dodgeball in school. Nobody likes to get picked last for dodgeball. It's almost like getting rejected. For those of you that might be younger and didn't get the chance to play dodgeball in school, it was basically a socially acceptable way to pick on and bully other kids through humiliation and physical violence. Getting pick last sucked. It was like a denial.

Loan denials are not a very fun part of the loan process. Let's be realistic for a moment. Not every person that applies for loan is going to get approved. There are several reasons why someone would be turned down. All of the underwriting criteria we talked about in chapter 6 is a good starting point to figure out why someone shouldn't get a loan.

We mentioned in chapter 8 that strong policies and procedures help reduce fair lending risk. That can be restated here.

If a bank has good underwriting procedures in place
and they are consistently followed,
there is little denial risk left over.

That doesn't always happen, which is why this chapter exists.

Doing It The Right Way

Let's get back to the legal and illegal forms of discrimination for a moment. A bank can legally deny a loan because of somebody's credit score. We have long ago established that fact. However, a bank cannot legally deny a loan because of somebody's race. It should be easy to connect those two points and say that if a bank only uses legal criteria to make the credit decision, that criteria is very well defined, and they never stray from it, they should have very little denial risk. In theory, that's correct. Oh, if we could just get people to follow the rules, right?

The loan denial process has a lot of technical requirements laid out by rules and regulations. There are time frames in which a lender must follow in order to even make a loan decision. Banks can't sit on an application for months and make you wait on a decision. There are also several forms that they need to fill out and send when they deny a loan application. While those are an important part of the denial process, they are technical in nature. We are not going to bore you with those details. Instead, let's revisit an earlier topic – discouraging applications.

Discouraging Applicants

In chapter 4, we introduced some risks that are present during the application process. When a loan officer prescreens applicants to see if they would qualify before actually filling out a formal application, they are going down a dangerous path. What ends up happening is that a lender makes an informal decision that an applicant likely isn't going to qualify for a loan, and they talk them out of actually going through the application process. This happens all the time.

You may be asking yourself how is it possible for somebody to find out if a lender is discouraging applications? We introduced this a bit already, but we will dive a little deeper here.

The first way is not necessarily the easiest, but it can help tell the story. We mentioned this briefly already, but it's using the secret shopper. If someone suspected a bank or specific loan officers of discouraging applications, they can send a secret shopper to verify. This is usually a person who falls into a higher risk prohibited basis group that goes through the process of applying for a loan.

They would want to give information to the lender that is likely not going to qualify them to see if the lender discourages them from applying. Discouraging applications is a big no-no. Loan officers should encourage all applicants to apply and let the underwriting process happen so that they get a fair and consistent decision, not one on-the-fly that the loan officer is likely guessing on.

Regulatory agencies also conduct interviews with lenders. It's called the fair lending interview, and I've done many of them. Oftentimes you can learn through a fair lending interview that lenders are likely discouraging applicants. I know what you might be thinking: There is no way that a loan officer is going to admit to discrimination in a fair lending interview with a federal bank regulator, right? Actually, it happens all of the time. Why? Because they often don't know their behavior is discriminatory, so they just don't know they are doing anything wrong. That sounds like a training opportunity for that lender to me.

Looking at the Data

For certain banks that have to report all of their home loan applications, it's a bit easier. The Home Mortgage Disclosure Act requires certain lenders to record all home loan applications they receive each year. During the application process, the lender will have to ask many questions to the applicant. Some of those questions are the race, sex, ethnicity, age, and marital status of the applicants. The average person may look at that questionnaire and wonder why their bank or mortgage company is asking for that information. They may even think that the lender will use that as a basis to discriminate against them. That cannot be further from the truth. Certain lenders are required to collect that data on all applications and report it annually to the federal government. Bank examiners will then review that information to ensure that a lender is not discriminating against certain applicants.

Providing your personal demographic information on home loan applications actually helps prevent discrimination, not promote it.

Banks that have to collect HMDA data are not collecting it on the LOANS they make but the APPLICATIONS they take. They are collecting data on every application they receive. Yes, those applications that end up in a loan will of course be reported. However, every other application that does not ultimately end up in a loan is also reported. The most common examples of applications that don't end up in loans are those withdrawn because the applicant changed their mind or went with a different lender and those that are denied. How does this help find institutions who are discouraging applications?

By simply looking at the number of denied applications in their data, it is pretty easy to figure out when a lender is under-reporting denied applications. Lenders will be compared to other lenders in their same area – they call this peer data. This is a great way for an auditor or examiner to compare banks in the same area to see if there are outliers.

If one lender has substantially less denials than another lender, but they make a similar number of loans, that's a red flag.

I have already hinted at this process, but what a loan officer will do is have interviews with applicants before they officially fill out an application. They will ask questions like their income, current debt payments, and an estimate of their credit score. If the loan officer thinks that the applicant is likely going to get denied, they will talk them out of ever applying.

Why would a lender want to do that? First of all, it saves the loan officer a lot of work. If you have ever had the pleasure of buying (or refinancing) a home, you may remember that two-foot-tall stack of documents and disclosures that you had to "read" and sign. I know most people don't ever read them. They just want to know what their payment is and when it's due. I'm one of the lucky few who gets to read all of those for a living.

All of that paperwork takes time. Even if the loan is denied, lenders still have a lot of paperwork that they need to do. If they can discourage somebody who they don't think will be approved anyway, they save themselves a lot of effort for a loan that they believe will never be approved. I'm not picking on lenders. I'm just hinting at human nature.

A bank's rate of denials can be compared to other lenders. If only one bank does it the right way and actually encourages all applicants to go through the process as they should and reports all of their denials, they may stand out as an outlier of being a lender that denies more applications than everyone else. In a perfect world, all banks do their job and report all applications.

Banks that discourage applications can throw off the data for everyone else.

All of this home loan data gets reported every year and is thoroughly reviewed by the bank's internal compliance and audit staff. The data is then reviewed and tested by bank examiners to ensure that it is accurate and that it can be relied upon for future fair lending examinations.

If a bank has too many errors and issues in their home loan data, they could be forced to reverify every piece of data they reported. What would that process look like? I'm glad you asked because it's not cheap, quick, or easy. As of 2022, there are 110 pieces of information to report on every home loan application. If we were to take those 110 pieces of data and multiply that by 100 home loan applications, my public-school education tells me that is 11,000 pieces of data that has to be reviewed.

The average loan file can be more than 400 pages long. That means that someone (usually some poor compliance guy like me) has to dig through hundreds of pages to find and verify those pieces of data. A bank that takes 10,000 applications a year has more than a million pieces of data to review. You can see how expensive and time consuming that can get. It's in a bank's best interest to collect the data and report it right the first time. I've seen banks that have had to reverify all of their home loan data, and not one has claimed to enjoy the process.

Comparative File Analysis

Another way a bank can test their data to ensure that they are making fair loan decisions is through a comparative file analysis. This is a reactive measure. It doesn't prevent discrimination; it only helps identify it after the fact. The basic idea behind a comparative file analysis is that it takes loans that were approved and compares them to applications that were denied. Using underwriting factors as a guide, an auditor can re-create loan decisions to find out if lenders are following procedures and treating people fairly and consistently for specific loan products.

You take one piece of criteria and compare it to the rest. It sounds complicating, but it's actually fairly straight forward.

Let's use an easy example – credit score. If I wanted to find out if a bank is discriminating when making car loan decisions, I can use the applicant's credit score as a starting point. I will go through all of the denied applications and find the best credit score that the bank ever denied for a car loan (in whatever period we choose, say a 1-year timeframe).

Let's say that the best credit score of any applicant that was denied in that year was 650. I then would look through all the approved car loans and find out what is the worst credit score that was approved. Let's say that worst credit score approved was 600. I now have my best denied applicant (650 credit score) and worst approved applicant (600 credit score). Every other car loan applicant that was denied that had a credit score between 600 and 650 would be my sample.

I would then look at all of the other underwriting characteristics that the lender considered to determine if the applicants were treated fairly. I don't like forcing people to do math, so I'll use an easy example and do it for you. Let's say our applicants are applying for a $10,000 car loan. Let's also say that our worst approved loan (that person who got the car loan with the 600-credit score) put $5000 down.

That would mean that they had a loan-to-value ratio of 50%. Since most people tend to borrow 100% of the money that they need when they buy a car (100% loan-to-value), 50% is really good for the lender. That greatly reduces their risk of loss if they have to repossess the car and sell it if the borrower doesn't pay back the loan.

Now we compare that to all of the denied applicants who had a better credit score than our worst approved (our 600-credit score person). Let's argue for a moment that all of the denied applicants in our sample had loan-to-value ratios of 100%. This could be one explaining factor of why they got denied for these car loans even though they had a better credit score than our worst approved.

An auditor can follow the same logic and methodology with any underwriting criteria. Simply find the worst approved and best denied to find the sample. Then look at the other characteristics to see if the decisions make sense. This can be a very manual process, but banks can purchase software that automates this and does the review in a matter of minutes.

Real-World Example

I once did a bank examination for a bank that had to collect all of the home loan data we talked about earlier. While analyzing the raw data, we saw that this bank had a denial rate to African-American borrowers for mobile home loans at 90%. Is that good or bad? Well, that depends. We needed a comparison to determine if that is a red flag. We used the denial rates to white borrowers as the control. What we found was that the denial rates to white borrowers for the same product was 50%. There was no other explanation as to why denial rates were so much higher to a particular prohibited basis group. As a result, we had to do a comparative file analysis. Unfortunately, we could not automate this part of the analysis. Poor Tory had to do it all by hand – it took two weeks. I'm still thinking about it.

I combed through every approved and denied application for every possible underwriting criterion and found our best denied and worst approved in every category. I then looked at all of the other factors to determine if loan decisions were fair and consistent or potentially on a prohibited basis. I will tell you this is not a fun process. This is not fun for the regulators and is certainly not fun for the bankers.

Fortunately, this bank had strong policies and procedures in-place. They made consistent and fair loan decision, they rarely went outside of loan policy, and we (as reviewers of the data) were able to recreate all of the loan decisions. In the end, we were able to prove this bank was not discriminating. All of the approval and denial decisions were based on legal underwriting factors and not on a prohibited basis. The lesson? Strong policies and procedures, consistently followed, help reduce fair lending risk.

Building Prevention into the Denial Process

The process starts with the application. Have consistent application procedures. A loan officer should never discourage an applicant from applying. Give everyone the same chance to go through the underwriting process. Sometimes, a piece of information sounds bad in a conversation and may sound like it will lead to a denial, but when the underwriting process is allowed to take place, it doesn't stop the loan from being made.

Don't go the extra mile for one applicant and not the other. If you are willing to consider additional information or let an applicant pay down other debt (because their debt-to-income ratio is too high), or allow them to pay off a judgment on a credit bureau report, be willing to do that for everyone. Too often we see a loan officer go above and beyond for an applicant to get them approved for a loan. There's nothing wrong with that. The problem is they don't do that for everyone, thus treating people differently on a prohibited basis.

Finally, consistently follow procedures and minimize exceptions. I know I sound like a broken record here, but when loan officers follow procedures every time, risk goes down. Procedures are there for a reason. One, to make sure loan officers make safe and sound loans. Two, to make sure loan officers make loans consistently and fairly. Not following procedures throws that all out the window and risk goes through the roof.

Chapter Takeaways

- Put good procedures in place during the application process.
- Train loan staff to not discourage applicants.
- Consistently follow underwriting guidelines to reduce denial risk.
- Perform a comparative file analysis when anomalies show up in the data.

The Details

I don't wish a comparative file analysis on anyone. If you can automate the process through software, by all means, go for it. Software can make your life much easier, and this is one of the areas where it has the most impact. Personally, I'm not a fan of performing a file analysis just for the sake of doing them. They are a lot of work, don't always tell us anything useful, and often times other anomalies show up that are not issues, but now you have to chase down those rabbit holes to explain them. I know examiners are pushing more and more for them, but ask them why? Is there an actual risk that you believe this will help identify, or do you want it done for the sake of doing it?

If you are a regulator, it's time to start thinking why we are starting fair lending examinations with a file analysis. The problem with this method of thinking is that there are so many areas that should be reviewed first. If underwriting criteria is strong and always followed, a file analysis should never be needed. There should always be a reason for doing this review, and it should be because of a breakdown in the compliance management system or because of HMDA data that shows negative trends that cannot otherwise be explained.

CHAPTER TEN

Marketing Risk

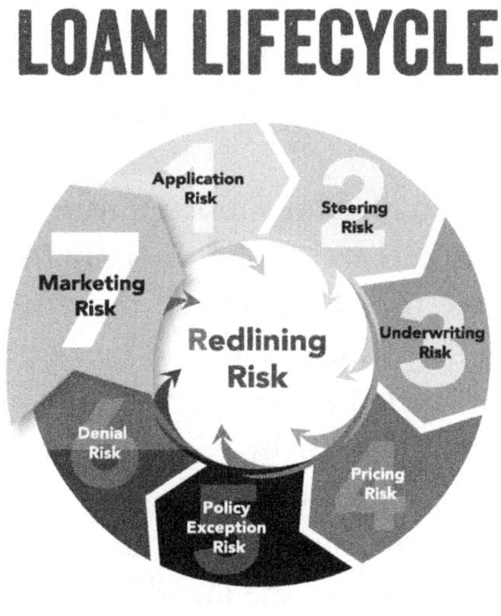

Imagine driving down the highway in an American city. You look to your right and there is a large billboard with a family on it. Mom, dad, and 2.1 kids are standing on the lawn in front of a house smiling. You know, the "Typical American Family." This was clearly an advertisement for a bank wanting to sell you a home loan. You look to the upper right of the billboard, and there is a big arrow pointing down at the family that says "We want people like YOU as our neighbors." Oh, and the people in the picture just happen to be a white family.

I still cringe every time I think of that billboard. What type of message is that sending? Are they meaning that they are marketing to young families to be their home loan lender, or are they sending a message of the kind of people they want living in their neighborhoods? The intent behind the ad is irrelevant. What is relevant is the message it is actually sending to the community.

What is a person of color supposed to feel when they see that ad? Will they feel welcomed to apply for a home loan at that bank since they don't match the profile of "people like YOU" from the billboard? Would they even want to live in that neighborhood? I realize this story sounds a bit far-fetched, but it's true. It actually happened and was the focus of a federal bank examination.

Marketing is really our last risk in the loan life cycle. However, when it comes to the loan lifecycle, marketing often technically comes first. I put this at the end because I wanted to introduce you to the other risks so you can see how each of them can apply to how banks market their products and services.

When you think marketing, think any message a bank puts out to the industry to try to gain customers.

This is often a bank's first contact with a potential customer. As technology evolves, so do the ways in which a bank can market their products and services. Even as recent as the year 2000, many banks used newspaper marketing as a primary way to get their message out. For our younger readers, a newspaper was basically the internet printed on paper that turned your fingers black. Radio was also very common for smaller institutions. If a bank was large enough, they could afford TV commercials.

Today, news organizations have transitioned to online news content. Commercial radio is not near as popular as it once was, and a growing majority of people don't even watch traditional TV anymore. Marketing has evolved, and the banking industry has evolved with it. New opportunities now exist for banks to really target the people they want to market to. While these new marketing channels provide great benefit, they bring with them a great deal of risk.

A Picture is Worth a Thousand Words

The first thing a bank must consider is when it includes pictures of people in marketing materials. Do the people or actors in the advertisement represent the people that live in the market area? I once did a review where I looked at a bank's home loan marketing materials and their website. I must've looked at nearly 50 pictures of people (basically actors/models) and found only a single person of color represented in all of their marketing materials.

This same bank had a market presence in a large city, but not a single bank branch was anywhere near a high minority neighborhood. When we looked at their home loan data, they were taking applications and making loans to minority applicants at a rate five times less than everyone else. It's hard to imagine that when this institution had no branches anywhere near minority populations and all of their marketing materials were of white actors, that any minorities are walking in the door.

Targeted Marketing

The next thing a bank needs to consider is what marketing channels they use. There are a lot of new ways to get a message out there.

Through social media and targeted search marketing, a bank can specifically market to any single person they want. This is where many banks get into trouble.

What they will try to do is target certain individuals based on certain characteristics. That makes sense if you think about it. If you want to market student loans, you want to target students. If you want to market home equity loans, you want to target people who own a home. The problem? When they choose the criteria of people to market to, those characteristics are often a prohibited basis.

Let's expand a bit more on student loans. If you are the head of marketing for a bank that offers student loans, who would you think is your target market? I would think to market to people ages 18 to 26. You could find the ages of people online and make sure they are the ones that saw your ads. Companies do this all of the time. Why is banking any different? Because age is a prohibited basis group under the law. If you target market based on age, you are discriminating against those outside the age group you are targeting.

Ironically, seniors are one of the fastest growing populations when it comes to student loan debt. And by seniors, I don't mean college seniors; I mean seniors citizens. Many grandparents are co-signing for grandkids to help pay for college. The amount of student loan debt for retired individuals is climbing every day, so does it even make sense to market based on age?

Credit cards for college students is another area that historically has caused many problems. While we don't see it as often anymore, credit card banks used to target college students because they were not financially sophisticated and often didn't even understand what they were signing up for. Many young college students would apply for a credit card, run up debt, and then destroy their credit. Banks were targeting them because they were profitable – and they were targeting them simply because of their age.

You also can target market by neighborhoods. Using targeted marketing through different social media sites and search engines, a bank can pick where people live and determine who they want to see their ads simply by the neighborhood's customers live in. For years, banks have focused on certain neighborhoods to make loans while totally excluding others.

Spoiler alert: the neighborhoods usually left off of the marketing lists are high minority areas.

Real-World Example

This same concept has been around for many years before internet marketing existed. Banks used to send marketing mailers to only certain neighborhoods. They would target high income and white neighborhoods and basically just exclude higher minority areas.

During a bank examination, I once had the head of a bank's marketing department tell me that it was bank policy to not send home loan marketing materials to a particular ZIP code. When I looked to see where that ZIP code was, I found out that it was a Native American reservation. That institution was purposely avoiding home loans in a high minority area. One of the ways they avoided lending to those residents was by not marketing to them.

One of the easiest ways that most banks get in trouble is that either the marketing department does not understand these basic principles because they have not been trained or they simply have not reviewed their marketing program for fair lending risks.

Tying In Other Risks

Marketing risk crosses over with several of the other risks we have already talked about. Steering risk is a great example. We have seen banks that target market minority applicants only with their highest cost products. They will send marketing materials for Loan Product C (highest interest rates and fees) only to certain individuals or neighborhoods.

Minority individuals end up getting a disproportionate amount of the worst loan products, and marketing is a major contributing factor.

I have seen banks target market a certain segment of the population that doesn't primarily speak English. There is nothing wrong with creating marketing materials in another language to try and give those individuals access to credit. The problem comes in when they only market their worst products to that population. This leads to steering risk and discrimination because a large majority of individuals who get those highest cost loan products are non-English speaking and share a common prohibited basis group characteristic such as race or ethnicity.

We also see targeted marketing crossover with pricing risk. Those same individuals that were targeted for the highest cost loan products are now going to pay a much higher rate of interest and fees, on average, than white borrowers. We're starting to see how all of these risks come together. If a bank targets a certain area or group of people with their highest cost products, there is a high probability of discrimination on at least one or more prohibited basis groups. You can see now why I put marketing at the end of the cycle.

Marketing can greatly increase or reduce fair lending risk, but banks have to understand how it impacts everything they do. A bank's marketing team must be highly trained in their field, and these fair lending risks should be at the core of that training. The marketing materials that they create should always be reviewed by compliance professionals who have a strong understanding of fair lending laws and regulations.

The most successful banks have great working relationships between their marketing and compliance staff to help prevent and reduce fair lending risks.

Social Media Marketing

I want to end this chapter by digging deeper into social media use. The first issue is when a loan officer tries to create their own marketing messages outside of the normal approved marketing channels. I do not mind employees trying to go above and beyond in the pursuit of bringing in new business and customers. As a small business owner, I can appreciate that. The problem is that the banking industry is so highly regulated that it takes somebody with an extensive knowledge in compliance to make sure marketing messages follow the rules and are free of potential discrimination.

When a loan officer goes off on their own to create marketing messages for social media, they don't understand all the ways they can get their bank in trouble.

With good training and a good social media policy, this can be avoided. But banks create social media messages all of the time, and employees can share those messages. This also creates risk.

Most banks that I've worked with have good procedures in place to create and approve compliant marketing materials. The normal process we see is that someone in the marketing department will create the materials and they will be posted on social media. That's a pretty common way of handling marketing and fairly safe. The problem is when a loan officer or other employee shares that social media posts, they may add their own thoughts and calls to action to that post, and that's what gets them into trouble. The average bank employee doesn't have a deep knowledge of compliance and often creates issues when they try to add to a marketing message.

Employee Social Media Use

The other item I want to talk about is a much more unpopular topic that people often get sensitive about. That is what bank employees post on their own personal social media pages. The United States allows its citizens freedom of speech. That's guaranteed by law. However, that freedom comes with responsibility and consequences, and this is where the unpopular part comes in.

I've had people tell me before that they can say whatever they want online, and it should not have any impact on their employment. These people commonly work for industries that have rules and regulations on how their work should be done but little in the way of the types of discrimination laws we see in banking. Therefore, they can post political opinions, religious views, or anything else that they want and face little scrutiny because of their line of work.

Employees that work for banks also can say whatever they want. The difference is that the banking industry has laws and regulations on how to treat applicants fairly. Banking and lending are so highly regulated that people like me devote their entire lives just trying to help banks navigate all of the rules and regulations. Entire careers are built around the complexity of banking compliance.

When bank employees make comments that cross prohibited basis boundaries, even on their personal pages, those comments can be viewed as discriminatory and can create significant regulatory issues for their employer.

Real-World Example

During the 2020 election season, an employee of a small family-owned bank made a very polarizing comment on their own personal Facebook page. This employee made a horribly discriminatory comment about a political candidate. As with all social media posts, it's public. Not surprisingly, other members of the community saw the post and immediately took screenshots. For a small family-owned bank in a small town, this comment blew up big and fast.

As you might expect, the local news agencies picked up on this right away. They say there is no such thing as bad press, but people that say that don't work in the banking regulatory world. In fact, it was such a big deal that for weeks when you went to this bank's home page, there was a large banner across the very top that had a link to a page that was only there to address the comment and the backlash. That means that when you went to this bank's website, the first thing that you saw was that one of their employees made a terrible discriminatory comment.

What do you think that will do for the reputation of that bank? The ironic part of this story was that the employee who made the comment had nothing to do with lending. This person was a back-office employee and never made a loan or worked directly with customers.

All bank employees' actions online can have a significant impact on the reputational risk of their employer, as this bank learned the hard way.

Every bank should have a strong social media policy. Yes, most employers have a policy that says what you can do on your work computer and often includes using social media on company owned machines. That's not good enough anymore. A social media policy should inform employees what is acceptable behavior on social media and how social media comments can affect their employment. This is the unpopular part. I am all about free speech. I spent 20 years in the military defending it. But if you want to limit risk of discrimination as a bank, do not let your employees go there. It's a small sacrifice that people need to accept to work in a highly regulated industry such as banking.

Building Prevention into the Marketing Process

Say it with me – processes, procedures, and training. I know it's repetitive, but it's important, easy, and it works.

First of all, banks need a process to get marketing materials approved. I mentioned before and I will again, a bank's marketing and compliance staff need to have a good working relationship. Too often the compliance department gets labeled as the "No Department," but that's not the way it has to be. Working together to build good marketing materials free of potential discrimination is the best way to minimize risk.

Secondly, have policies in place about who can speak on behalf of the bank. Banks need to hold their employees responsible for their behavior online. Having a good social media policy is a big step. Too many times I've seen a great policy, but when I interview lenders, they tell me they haven't read it in seven years! Have employees read it every year and sign it. What good is a policy if nobody has read it?

Lastly, make sure the marketing department understands targeted marketing. A bank's marketing professionals need to understand that how they choose who sees the message has an impact on every loan life cycle risk we discussed. If a bank is going to target a certain group of people to see a marketing message, make sure it's not on a prohibited basis. In major bank discrimination cases, marketing issues typically are not the root cause. However, a bank's marketing efforts always add fuel to the discriminatory fire and only make a case worse. When a bank is getting hit with discriminatory violations, their marketing is often picked apart, and holes appear very quickly. A bank's marketing efforts are then criticized and become a contributor to the overall problem.

Chapter Takeaways

- Ensure marketing materials represent the people who live in your market area.
- Have compliance professionals do a secondary review of all marketing materials.
- Create a strong social media policy to guide all employees, and make sure they read it and sign it every year.
- Ensure the marketing team fully understands targeted marketing risk and that it's never done on a prohibited basis.

The Details

As banks grow, I see a shift in marketing strategy from more product-based marketing to brand imaging. Product-specific marketing is just as it sounds; you focus the ads more on the actual product itself. Brand imaging is more of promoting the brand of your bank. For instance: "We are the region's premier home loan lender" or "We serve the small business needs of our community."

There is nothing wrong with product-specific marketing, but it does carry more risk and needs more attention. When you talk about specific products, most notably loan products, there are more fair lending risks along with the other potential consumer protection laws and regulations that you deal with on a daily basis.

My theory is that bigger banks stick more with the brand imaging to control risk. Everyone knows bigger banks offer checking accounts, business loans, and home loans, so they try and position themselves more as an industry leader that participates in the community. Your bank should have a general marketing strategy and controls in place to support that strategy.

The other thing I want to mention is the continual growth of social media. It's so easy to create a social media account, start connecting with customers, and market directly to them. The biggest issue I see in doing bank audits is that marketing and compliance don't have a good idea of how people are chosen to see the bank's ads.

When I do fair lending audits, I do fair lending interviews with lenders and underwriters all of the time, but I also do a fair lending interview with the bank's marketing team. I can't tell you how many times they just don't know for sure how their targeted marketing really works and how people come across their ads. The scarier part is they usually rely upon a third-party company to help with social media marketing.

While those third parties have the best intentions in mind, if they are not familiar with banking laws and regulations, they may not know that how they are setting up the bank's marketing campaign is greatly increasing fair lending risk.

Your job as a compliance or audit professional is to ask questions and keep asking questions until you are 100% certain how your ad campaigns are working. You need to dig deep because if you don't, or even if you do, the examiners likely will too. You know as well as I do that you always want to find issues before the examiners do.

Part 3

BRINGING IT ALL TOGETHER

CHAPTER ELEVEN

Redlining Risk

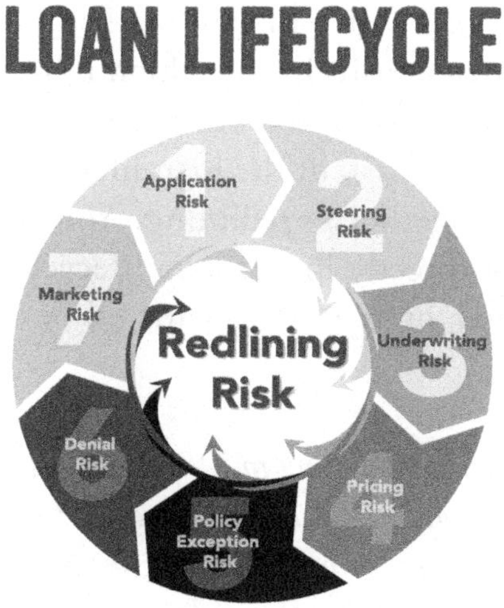

I picture early 20th century America when I think of redlining. I imagine some wealthy white banker in his three-piece suit, smoking a cigar, and looking at a map in his office of the city in which his bank operates. He's looking at where they are bringing in deposits and making loans, and maybe even where he wants to open a new bank branch. He also knows the neighborhoods and who lives in those neighborhoods.

Pretty much every metropolitan area in America has neighborhoods with higher percentages of minority residents. This old-school banker knew this. He did not want to make loans to minority people or in the areas they lived. He comes up with this idea of drawing lines around these high-minority areas with a big red marker to signify that his bank will not make loans in these high minority areas. This is how I imagine the term redlining was born.

Welcome to the risk in the loan lifecycle where we will tie everything together – redlining. You will notice that redlining is not directly in our loan lifecycle circle. In fact, it's in the center of the circle with all of the other risks pointing to it.

I've struggled with trying to fit redlining into the loan life cycle for years, until I finally realized that redlining is the product of all of the other risks combined into one major risk area.

Definition of Redlining

Every risk in the loan life cycle process can lead to redlining risk. In the simplest terms, it's the results of a breakdown in the lender's overall performance. So, what is redlining?

Here is the textbook definition: *Redlining is a form of illegal disparate treatment in which a lender provides unequal access to credit, or on unequal terms of credit, because of the race, color, national origin, or other prohibited characteristics of the residents of the area in which the credit seeker resides or will reside or in which the residential property to be mortgaged is located.*

If reading that definition does not make you want to quit your job and become a banking compliance professional, I don't blame you. We compliance professionals are a special breed of weird, but let's get back on topic. What does that definition really mean? Here's Tory's definition.

It basically means that a bank is not lending to certain people or areas, and the reason is pretty much always because of a prohibited basis characteristic. Either a bank simply doesn't lend to certain high minority neighborhoods, they will lend to those neighborhoods but rarely, or they target certain neighborhoods with higher costs loan products.

Geographic Footprint of Branches

There are a couple different concepts I want to discuss in this chapter, but they all tie together. I want to start with a concept that deals directly with banks, but other lenders, like payday lenders, mortgage companies, or any lending company with physical office locations can also be included: the geographic placement of bank branches and loan offices.

Where a bank places their physical offices will have a large impact on the types of applicants that apply for loans.

This is a very simple concept. If you place branches in predominantly white neighborhoods, you're going to get predominantly white applicants applying for loans. The same works with any population. If you have branches in neighborhoods with high Hispanic populations, you should expect to see a high percentage of applications coming from Hispanic borrowers. There is no fancy science behind this. This is simply the Law of Probability.

What banks have done in the past is strategically placed their branches away from higher minority neighborhoods. Sometimes it happens by accident while other times it is deliberate. The reason or intent doesn't matter; it is still redlining. The days of bankers drawing redlines on maps may be long gone, but redlining very much still exists in the 21st Century.

Social Breakdown of Cities

Let's expand on the branch location concept a bit more and introduce a new related concept. I didn't always dream of being a banking compliance professional. I know that's hard to believe, but when I was a teenager, I didn't dream of reading laws and regulations for a living. I wanted to be a professional baseball broadcaster. My dream job was (and still is) to be the color analyst for the Minnesota Twins radio broadcast. I wanted to sit next to John Gordon and call Twins baseball games. John is now retired, and I have absolutely no play-by-play experience, so that dream likely will just remain a dream. Why is that important to the story? That baseball part really isn't, but what is important is while studying communication and broadcasting, I also minored in sociology.

As an undergraduate student, I remember taking my first sociology course: Sociology 100. Really basic stuff, but also very eye-opening and relevant to this story. I remember the professor talking about the social and economic breakdowns of metro areas in the United States. I am certainly not a sociology expert, and I do not pretend to be. In fact, I don't even have sources to cite, so I'm just recalling this from memory. But I want to talk about this concept to help you form an understanding of how redlining and branching structures typically work and what the social impact is.

What Sociology 100 taught me was that the central portion of most major cities is the financial hub. This is where all the high-rise buildings are, it is where most of business and finance happens, and it is where most people go to work. You can easily see it when you look at any city skyline; it's easy to pick out. It's mostly commercial buildings without a lot of residents, although that's not always the case.

The few blocks that surround this area are often the poorest areas of the city. There is a lot of homelessness and sometimes higher minority populations. Once you move a few blocks out from that circle, you will see changes. You get out a few more blocks and you start to see shifts in income, poverty, and race. Eventually you get way out in the suburbs and you will see very little diversity in the populations.

This phenomenon is not so much a racial pattern as it is an economic pattern. We also learned about studies of cities where the populations in and around the downtown metro areas change over time. More than 100 years ago when the United States had huge influx of immigrant populations, the racial makeup of those neighborhoods was different than they are today. White immigrants from certain European countries would make up the poorest areas of the city. However, those white populations had key advantages that many U.S. citizens of color still lack today.

As the 20th century moved on, those poor white immigrants were given access to the financial industry. As a result, they were able to pay for college, buy a home, start a business, and build up their families out of generational poverty. They eventually moved out of those areas and new populations moved in, often people of color. Those new residents in the downtown areas of cities were not given the same access to credit, hence where redlining comes from and why it's such a powerful tool to keep certain groups of people from prosperity. Today, many of those neighborhoods are minority populations.

What some financial institutions have done is kept their branches outside of those areas and placed them in the predominantly white neighborhoods.

The term "horseshoe" is often used when looking at these branching structures. If you don't know what a horseshoe looks like it's much like the letter C. Imagine any downtown metropolitan area in the United States. Now imagine that all of a bank's branches surround that area in a half circle that looks like a horseshoe. Rather than putting branches in the high minority areas, they are in a horseshoe shape around the minority neighborhoods.

The whole idea behind branching structure problems is that branches are not in minority neighborhoods. As a result, they are not taking applications from minority individuals. As a result of that, minority individuals are not getting loans and don't have access to credit. There are ways to see if a lender has branching structure issues. The easiest way is to grab a map that shows minority populations and place a dot everywhere a bank has a branch.

If a bank's branches are nowhere near the high minority neighborhoods, there's a branching problem.

Finding Lending Activity

The next way is to actually plot applications and loans on a map. Oftentimes you need access to software in order to do this, or at least do it quickly. The home loan data that we talked about in previous chapters is often used to plot applications and loans. One of the pieces of information that every reporter of home loan data must collect is the neighborhood where the home is located. This allows for testing to see if a bank is making loans in high minority areas.

The concept of plotting loans is pretty simple and pretty much the same as looking at a branching structure. Imagine a map on the wall. Then take a little pin and place that in everywhere a bank makes a loan. Stand back and see if the pins are in high minority areas. This is really groundbreaking stuff, right? It's really no more complicated than that. Is a bank making home loans in high minority areas? You can apply the same concept with small business loans. We can look at all of the small business loans a bank makes in a year, plot them on a map, and see where they are.

Redlining is traditionally a home loan problem, but it can be applied to all loan types.

Tying in Other Risks

I mentioned that redlining is the product of all loan life cycle risks. Let's tie it back to marketing. When it comes to placing marketing in actual neighborhoods, I think of billboards. Where are a bank's billboards actually located? Are they in or around high minority areas or not? Does a bank send out mailers to customers in a certain area? If so, are they avoiding mailing ads to certain neighborhoods?

Let's talk about the application process. If a bank doesn't have branches in high minority areas, how many loan applications do you think they are taking from minority applicants? No applications = no loans. Not exactly groundbreaking stuff, is it?

What about steering risk? We mentioned in Chapter 5 that banks may target certain neighborhoods with their worst products. What if the high minority neighborhoods all get Loan Products B and C while the white neighborhoods are getting mostly Loan Product A?

Underwriting and pricing risks follow the same methodology. If you don't have strong procedures in place to make loan decisions, those decisions can often be made on a prohibited basis. As a result, residents in high minority neighborhoods are disproportionately harmed because a bank has a weak program in place. With poor underwriting procedures, high denial risk is right behind it.

If you've lived in the United States more than a few minutes, you will know that there are many parts of the country that have very low minority populations. Since redlining is typically an issue that follows race, these low minority areas tend to have lower risk when it comes to redlining.

Just because an area has lower populations of minorities doesn't mean there isn't redlining risk.

Larger cities are a lot more diverse. Redlining issues are much easier to spot in these areas. Whenever a bank wants to expand their branching structure, they should really have an understanding of the neighborhoods they are expanding into, or neighborhoods they may be missing. If a bank already avoids branches in higher minority areas, opening a new branch in a white neighborhood is only going to make the problem worse.

Of all of the risks we talk about in this book, redlining is the one that is constantly in the news. Just within the last few weeks while writing this book, two more cases were published. Lending institutions are paying big fines, they are being forced to open new locations, and they are spending heavily on new marketing and outreach programs because they are not lending in high minority areas.

Just like any law, ignorance of it is not an excuse. All banks need to be aware and understand their risk. If you don't find your own problems, someone else will.

Building Prevention into Redlining

Every loan life cycle risk can contribute to redlining issues. To avoid this, a bank should be looking at their branching structure. Simply plotting branches on a map of minority populations is a great start. What is a bank to do if they find their branches are avoiding high minority areas? Act!

Yes, opening a new branch is very expensive, and it's not something that can be done overnight. However, marketing can be. Start outreach programs in those neighborhoods. Build relationships with mortgage brokers, real estate agents, and community working groups to help make loans in high minority areas.

While opening a branch is difficult because you need a vault, tons of security features, and a large footprint to build, a loan production office is not. A loan production office requires some small office space, a sign, and a loan officer. This is a great way to start building a physical presence in areas where bank offices don't currently exist.

All banks that have to collect home mortgage data should be enlisting in software to analyze that data. Software is a great tool to not only plot your branches on a map, but your loans and applications. Yes, banks need to make loans in high minority areas, but they first need to get applications from people in those areas. Compare your bank's performance to peer data. Remember, peer data is all of the other home loan lenders in your area. If they are getting applications at a rate of four to five times what your bank is, you have problems.

How are you supposed to increase lending in minority areas when you're not getting applications?

There's a little "hard-to-swallow" pill on peer data that I likely should have discussed before nearing the end of this book, but I will mention now. When you compare your performance to peer data, it will show you how you are performing and if you are meeting the same application and loan levels as other lenders in your area. However, you still need to compare your data to demographic data. For example, if 30% of your community is Hispanic borrowers, and only 6% of your loans went to Hispanic borrowers, that means your performance is way behind demographic data. However, you may look at peer data and show that the average lender in your area is only making about 8% of their loans to Hispanic borrowers. That might bring you some temporary comfort knowing that your performance is similar to what other lenders are doing.

Here comes the hard-to-swallow pill:

Just because peers' performance is also terrible doesn't mean your poor performance is acceptable. You must consider the likely possibility that others are also redlining.

Finally, look back at your marketing. Is it inclusive of the population? Do you include people of all different racial and ethnic backgrounds? Are you marketing to all neighborhoods? Redlining is a major problem, but many solutions to that problem are actually quite simple.

Chapter Takeaways

- Know where your branches are located by plotting them on a map. Compare that to minority populations in your area.
- Consider plotting both loans and applications on a map to see if you are avoiding certain neighborhoods.
- Compare your performance to peer data using software.
- If you find poor performance, don't wait. Act!

The Details

Redlining is going to get much worse before it gets any better. The reason is that so many banks in the country are old. They have been in place for decades and many over a century. They are not just going to pick up and move their physical locations. That means that they need more out-of-the-box thinking on how to solve this problem. I've had several institutions take my fair lending course that have come back to me and discovered major redlining issues. They always ask me what to do, and my answer is always the same – act!

If you find yourself in this position, the worst thing you can do is bury your head in the sand and pretend the problem doesn't exist. I've seen high profile redlining cases that did not result from a regulatory examination. That means someone, other than the examiners, saw the problem and raised the red flag. Anyone with software and your HMDA data can do the analysis for you.

I do branch analyses all the time. Give me 30 minutes, and I can geocode all of your bank locations, find your area demographics, and see if your branching structure is avoiding high-minority census tracts. You need to do this analysis yourself because if you don't, the examiners will.

If you find issues, don't panic. Admit the problem, inform management and the Board, and get to work. Start with ideas for marketing. Do some outreach and start finding loans. If you find the issue yourself and take strong efforts to address it, your case will be viewed much more favorably than if you did nothing.

I will tell you that just doing marketing and outreach to the higher minority areas your branches are avoiding may not be enough. If your closest branch is 20 minutes away from higher minority areas, all the marketing in the world may not make an impact. Is it practical to think that someone will drive 20 minutes, pass multiple other lenders on the way, to drive all the way to your nearest branch to get banking services?

We need to be real about "appearing" to address redlining issues and actually doing something about it. Just showing you are marketing in redlined areas often times is not enough to make an actual impact.

CHAPTER TWELVE

Future And Emerging Risk

You no doubt saw some common themes in this book. You may have come to the end and are thinking to yourself that it's more complicated than this. We need statistical models, complex reviews, regression analysis, and all those other fancy terms to combat fair lending risk. I get it. I know I make it sound simple. That's because the concepts are simple:

Strong policies and procedures are the best way to start building a fair lending program.

Implementing it, on the other hand, is the challenge. I can sit here and talk all day about how a program is supposed to look, and you may be nodding along with me, but if banks don't take the time to build a solid program and exercise the discipline to stick with it, this problem will never go away.

Every bank should have guidance on the acceptable way to make a loan. That's only the first step. Strong policies and procedures are a great start, but having employees that actually follow them is the next crucial step. When a loan officer strays away from loan policy, it introduces fair lending risk. The more often they do it and the further away from policy they go, the more the risk increases. Training is the next step in the process.

If lenders aren't trained on how to carry out the process, what good is it?

Finally, strong banks monitor and audit their performance. Monitoring does not have to be super scientific. I have seen small banks simply grab a handful of loan files every month to see if lenders are following policy. There's nothing difficult about that, and it's not time-consuming. Larger banks need something a lot more sophisticated, and that often leads to software. Performing periodic audits is the last step in the process. Having a highly qualified individual that knows what they're looking for review a program at least once a year is a great way to identify and help prevent discrimination.

I've done more than 100 fair lending reviews in my life, and I hope to have many good years yet in front of me. I've taken my knowledge and experience and put it into my fair lending school. If you are a banker that is interested in learning how to do better fair lending reviews, you can check it out at www.tcuniversity.us.

Complaints

One last factor that most people don't think about is complaints. Nobody likes receiving complaints, but they should be viewed as feedback on the system. Fair lending complaints should be treated very seriously as they can point to a potential major breakdown in the system. I have seen one lending-related complaint become the entire focus of a regulatory fair lending review. Take them seriously and investigate them thoroughly.

Loan Servicing

There are new and emerging risks that we didn't discuss in this book. Loan servicing is a growing concern in the banking industry. Some borrowers (usually a certain prohibited basis group) are being targeted and treated differently in the repayment process. You may have wondered why I didn't cover loan servicing in this book. Yes, loan servicing is often tied into fair lending risk, but this book focused on the risks in the loan origination process. People getting their loans serviced already received a loan. If they are mistreated or discriminated against during the loan servicing process, that is also a major issue. That's another book for another day.

Appraisals

In addition, we have seen a growing concern in the appraisal process. Many home loan applicants of color have seen the appraised value of their homes go down significantly because they either live in high minority neighborhoods or the appraiser can easily see that a person of color lives in that home.

I've heard stories of a black applicant get an unusually low appraised value for their home. This person then "white-washed" his home and ordered his own independent appraisal. By white-washing, he basically removed everything from his home that would lead someone to believe a person of color lived there. When he got his own independent appraisal done, the value of his home went up more than 40 percent.

Fair lending issues are always evolving. They evolve with the times and technology. As a nation, we need to be educated on these issues. We need to push back on the lending industry as a whole to put simple processes in place to prevent discrimination. Reactive measures are not good enough. All financial institutions need to train their people and put simple processes in place to prevent these issues from ever happening.

I hope this is not all doom and gloom. If you are an average reader who wanted to learn more on this topic, I hope you will walk away with a much better understanding of how lending works. If you are a lender or a manager of a bank or other type of financial institution, I hope this opened your eyes and gave you ideas on how to build a stronger lending program. This book was not meant to scare, but educate. Fair lending does not have to be difficult. Through simple education, processes, and reviews, every bank can help prevent discrimination and allow everyone the same equal access to credit that we all deserve.

Made in the USA
Monee, IL
17 April 2023

31996676R00089